The Minneapolis & St. Louis Railway

For
Edward Wilkommen
With
All Best Wishes
Don. L. Hofsommer
8 June 2009

p. 185

The Minneapolis & St. Louis Railway

A Photographic History

Don L. Hofsommer

Author of *Minneapolis and the Age of Railways*

University of Minnesota Press
Minneapolis · London

Frontispiece: Airbrushed publicity photograph proclaimed the great self-confidence of the Minneapolis & St. Louis Railway at the end of World War II.

Illustrations in the book are from the author's collection, and photographs in "A Fresh Approach?" and "End of the Line" were taken by the author unless credited otherwise.

Published by the University of Minnesota Press
111 Third Avenue South, Suite 290, Minneapolis, MN 55401-2520
http://www.upress.umn.edu

Library of Congress Cataloging-in-Publication Data

Hofsommer, Donovan L.
  The Minneapolis & St. Louis Railway : a photographic history / Don L. Hofsommer.
    p.   cm.
  ISBN 978-0-8166-5131-3 (hc : alk. paper) — ISBN 978-0-8166-5132-0 (pb : alk. paper)
  1. Minneapolis & St. Louis Railway—History. 2. Minneapolis & St. Louis Railway—Pictorial works. I. Title. II. Title: Minneapolis and St. Louis Railway.
  HE2791.M663H637 2009
  385.0973—dc22

                                                                                2008048902

Design and production by Mighty Media, Inc.
Text design by Chris Long

Printed in the United States of America on acid-free paper

The University of Minnesota is an equal-opportunity educator and employer.

16 15 14 13 12 11 10 09   10 9 8 7 6 5 4 3 2 1

For Frank P. Donovan Jr.

Contents

Preface

It was *my* railroad. Well, no, I owned none of the stock or any of the bonds issued by the Minneapolis & St. Louis Railway Company, but I took a proprietary interest in the road nevertheless. After all, I was born at Lutheran Hospital, nearly in sight of M&StL's yard at Fort Dodge; I lived at various times in communities along its lines (Callender, Fort Dodge, Spencer, Mason City, and Albert Lea); and I spent a summer as an M&StL section laborer. Its employees indulged me with innumerable trips in locomotive cabs, overnight stays in cabooses, and endless hours in depot offices where I inhaled a blizzard of yarns and embroidery spun by master storytellers who relished an enthusiastic audience. And I devoured every page of Frank P. Donovan's spritely Mileposts on the Prairie, marveling at M&StL's curious history and rejoicing at the road's more recent success under Lucian C. Sprague. Happily for me, Donovan became a friend—arguably the kindest and most generous person I have known—and a willing if unofficial mentor when I struggled to turn out a passable master's thesis. Frank died before he was able to do any followup to Mileposts, but I continued to dream that dream. After a very long gestation period, I was able to bring out three books that supplement Frank's Mileposts: The Tootin' Louie: A History of the Minneapolis & St. Louis Railway; The Hook & Eye: History of the Iowa Central Railway; and Minneapolis and the Age of Railways. I have every great hope that these books are work that he would approve of as additional tribute to the men and women of "our" railroad.

The pages that follow offer an illustrated excursion of M&StL's lifetime. I am greatly indebted to several persons who assisted me over the years by locating, lending, or donating photographs and other illustrations. These include Todd Orjala, Pieter Martin, Frank P. Donovan Jr., Rex C. Beach, Dennis E. Holmes, Paul H. Stringham, Scott D. McGinnis, Edward Wilkommen, Vern Wigfield, Vaughn R. Ward, Robert Kolbe, Alfred Tietel, H. Roger Grant, Aaron Isaacs, Harold Davidson, L. W. Andreessen, Robert Milner, Gordon E. Lloyd, James G. LaVake, Ernest Lehmann, Basil W. Koob, James Reuber, and especially William F. Armstrong and William D. Middleton.

All aboard!

Protecting Home Turf

Minneapolis Builds a Railway
1871–1899

THE EARLIEST CORPORATE LINKAGE to what became the Minneapolis & St. Louis Railway Company (M&StL) derived from a broad if ill-defined plan for prospective Minnesota roads during territorial days of the early 1850s, but nothing really happened until 1869 and 1870 when an old charter was dusted off and amended to create M&StL. The purposes of the road were implied in its very title: to connect Minneapolis with St. Louis by iron rail over a vertical axis route that would, proponents argued, obviate the already existing and very vigorous roads emanating from the lake port cities of Milwaukee and Chicago—roads that were, complained local advocates of M&StL, rapaciously encroaching on the "natural territory" of Minneapolis.

Business and manufacturing interests at Milwaukee and Chicago had, to be sure, embraced rails as a principal weapon in their campaign of urban economic imperialism calculated to spread dominance to the west and northwest. And leaders at Minneapolis had been inexplicably slow to comprehend all of this and to act affirmatively on their own account. Yes, nearby St. Anthony, to which Minneapolis soon would be joined, had gained railroad service in 1862 when Minnesota's pioneer road, St. Paul & Pacific, placed in service its ten-mile route up from St. Paul, but that road soon scurried off to the interior of the state and beyond. Additional service came in 1865 when a predecessor of Chicago, Milwaukee & St. Paul punched a branch into Minneapolis from its main route starting in St. Paul and running southward to Austin that, with connecting friendly lines in Iowa and Wisconsin, forged the state's first route eastward to Milwaukee and eventually to Chicago. However, Minneapolis was a mere way station on one road and at the stub end of the other. This was intolerable. M&StL was the proper antidote—a rail route from Minneapolis to St. Louis.

There was not a railroader among those who joined in founding M&StL. They were lumbermen, flour millers, politicians, and bankers—men such as John S. Pillsbury, Henry Titus Welles, and brothers William D. and Cadwallader C. Washburn—who finally sought to circumvent the power of Milwaukee and Chicago and their railroads with a Minneapolis-based system of their own. M&StL's purposes were clear enough, but M&StL's directors additionally worked to create an important subsidiary, Minneapolis & Duluth (M&D), in order to link

Minneapolis to the head of the Great Lakes at Duluth. M&D, said the Washburns and others, would offer a seasonal chute to the Great Lakes chain and create yet another means of short-circuiting Milwaukee and Chicago and at the same time gain access to impressive timber stock for the lumber mills at St. Anthony Falls.

But money was scarce and distressingly competitive. Aspirations for Minneapolis & Duluth were truncated accordingly. It would be driven northeasterly from Minneapolis to White Bear Lake, about fourteen miles, to a junction with the already completed Lake Superior & Mississippi (LS&M), which owned a route between St. Paul and Duluth. Service on M&D began in 1871. At the same time, construction crews on M&StL pressed southwestward through Cedar Lake and down a brow of bluffs into the valley of the Minnesota River to Chaska and Carver to meet St. Paul & Sioux City's diagonal line from the state capital into Iowa.

Money became the bugaboo. Jay Cooke and the fabled Northern Pacific (NP) appeared as white knights. M&StL and M&D both were leased to Lake Superior & Mississippi, which itself was leased by Northern Pacific. And Cooke and Northern Pacific acknowledged interest in support of other enterprises in Iowa and Missouri that collectively might make good on the Minneapolis-to-St. Louis dream. But it was not to be. Northern Pacific headed west across Minnesota from Duluth into Dakota Territory ahead of demand, Cooke and NP foundered, the Panic of 1873 came on, and leases were abrogated. M&StL and M&D again were independent—adrift, really, with unmet aspirations, without adequate financial backing to act on those aspirations, and greatly threatened by the vicious and ongoing national depression.

In time a new messianic figure appeared in the form of Burlington, Cedar Rapids & Northern (BCR&N), an aspiring organization that held a strategic route beginning on the Mississippi River in southeast Iowa at Burlington and running toward the northwest—tapping Cedar Rapids, Waterloo, Cedar Falls, and terminating near the Iowa–Minnesota boundary. BCR&N, with backing from much larger Chicago, Burlington & Quincy (CB&Q) and Chicago, Rock Island & Pacific (CRI&P or Rock Island), boasted favorable connections to both St. Louis (via CB&Q) and Chicago (via CB&Q or CRI&P) and presently proposed to cooperate with M&StL on financial matters to build to a connection with M&StL and to forge mutually beneficial traffic agreements. Eyes brightened in Minneapolis. On November 12, 1877, M&StL reached Albert Lea, 107 miles south of Minneapolis; passenger and freight operations between Minneapolis and St. Louis began soon thereafter with M&StL, BCR&N, and CB&Q in partnership.

Meanwhile, M&StL acted on its own in joining with romantic-sounding Fort Dodge & Fort Ridgely Railroad & Telegraph Company to open a 103-mile extension from Albert Lea to Fort Dodge, Iowa (completed midsummer 1880), and then pressed on a few miles farther to coalfields in and about Kalo. Construction crews rested only briefly before following engineer's stakes leading to even larger coal beds around Angus.

M&StL's new line into Iowa would produce wheat for the insatiable needs of flour millers at St. Anthony Falls and a marvelously expanded market for Minneapolis lumber millers, providing loads in both directions, a proper prescription for the road's financial health. Moreover, M&StL could fetch coal for the fuel-starved Northwest.

At about the same time, M&StL joined with St. Paul & Duluth (StP&D, successor to Lake Superior & Mississippi) to drive a new route from Minneapolis northeastward to Taylor's Falls, Minnesota, on the St. Croix River.

Additional reach came in 1881 when M&StL determined to move westward from Minneapolis on a carefully crafted crescent-shaped alignment above the Minnesota River that would take the road to the new or aspiring communities of Norwood, Arlington, Gaylord, and Winthrop. An important sidebar to this enterprise was tapping beautiful Lake Minnetonka and its fashionable resorts. Indeed, M&StL took a half interest in the Lake Park Hotel, and M&StL's president, W. D. Washburn, was owner of the *City of St. Louis*, an elegant 150-foot steamer placed on the lake during the early summer of 1881.

M&StL owned a curiously configured route structure, although each one of its constituent lines made sense in terms of generating traffic to and from the headquarters city of Minneapolis. Its line down to Albert Lea was an attractive strategic avenue, and its primacy in the west bank milling area of Minneapolis was a plum. Others took notice, especially Rock Island. Under the leadership of the talented Ramsom R. Cable, Rock Island was in an expansive mood, first taking lease of Burlington, Cedar Rapids & Northern and then, with a consortium of persons allied with CRI&P, gathered stock control of M&StL and with it M&D. "The Great Rock Island Route," as CRI&P was called in the 1880s, had in the process exploded into the Northwest— in its traditional style doing so by taking control rather than by constructing new. But Cable saw BCR&N and M&StL as launching pads for greater aspirations—a means to prove up on the "Pacific" in its corporate title by way of a northwest passage. To that end BCR&N construction crews in 1884 pushed northwestward out of Iowa, and M&StL crews labored westward out of the Minnesota River valley to a meeting at Watertown, Dakota Territory. From there they would move on, according to multiple reports, to Bismarck and potentially to points farther west. The "Albert Lea Route" (CRI&P, BCR&N, M&StL) was integral to all of it.

Cable and Rock Island had burst like comets onto the railway landscape of the Northwest. Cable predictably had no interest in the M&StL route to Taylor's Falls; it was given up to St. Paul & Duluth. But Cable did arrange to get M&StL into St. Paul, the state capital and an important transportation center by any standard. Not surprisingly, other contestants did not welcome Cable and Rock Island. Rate wars raged, and Cable and "The Great Rock Island Route" (and certainly M&StL) came out worse for the wear. Cable and Rock Island eventually lost interest and refocused on expansion to the south, southwest, and west; M&StL fell into receivership.

Matters bumped along uncertainly. Even before the Rock Island era, M&StL

had pushed a bit farther into Iowa, tapping the rich coalfields around Angus, connecting there with short line Des Moines & Fort Dodge. That road was soon leased to Rock Island, and then M&StL trains rolled on to Des Moines through a trackage rights agreement. Rumors had M&StL expanding elsewhere, to Kansas City perhaps, but that did not happen. In Minnesota, CRI&P succeeded in obtaining the lease of Wisconsin, Minnesota & Pacific for M&StL. Wisconsin, Minnesota & Pacific owned a route from Red Wing, on the Mississippi River south of St. Paul, to Mankato, on the Minnesota River to the west, that intersected at right angles M&StL's Minneapolis–Albert Lea artery at Waterville.

Rock Island investors and managers assumed that they would hold onto M&StL through reorganization, but in 1894 a group of New Yorkers wrested control. Their purposes for the property were unclear. Would they gussy up the road for marriage to a larger road? Would they aim for long-term independence? Whatever course would be embraced would derive from Edwin Hawley, the new president, and about whom little was known.

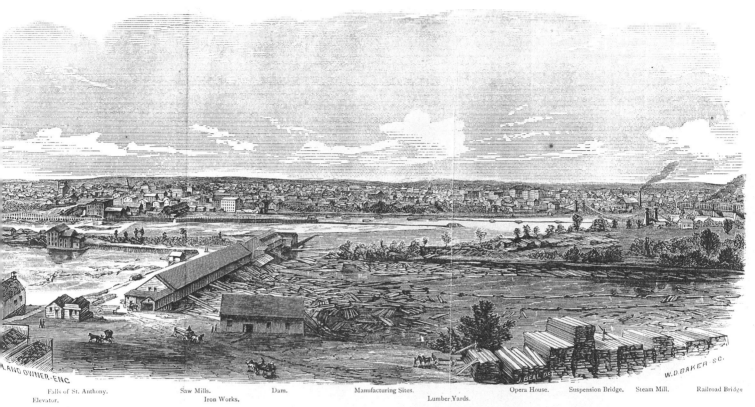

Falls of St. Anthony.   Saw Mills.   Dam.   Manufacturing Sites.   Opera House.   Suspension Bridge.   Steam Mill.   Railroad Bridge

Elevator.   Iron Works.   Lumber Yards.

MINNEAPOLIS, MINN.—ITS WATER-POWER, BUILDINGS, REAL ESTATE AND THE FALLS OF ST. ANTHONY.

The western bank of the Mississippi River at Minneapolis evolved into an industrial bonanza for M&StL, which dominated the area for several years.

Construction to the south from Minneapolis was depressingly slow. Finally crews pressed out of the Minnesota River valley to traverse young glacial plain typified by lakes and moraines. Bridging the Minnesota River at Carver was a challenge.

Manchester Locomotive Works delivered 0-4-0 number 50 late in 1881. It would be used in switching service, especially in the west bank milling district at Minneapolis.

Snow has not deterred the two women in the foreground of this view, who pause to witness the passing of this northbound freight near Waterville.

The handsome village of Jordan, thirty-two miles out from Minneapolis on the line to Albert Lea, provided a splendid volume of passengers and freight for M&StL. The crew of this caboose hop soon will be at work switching cars for local industry. SCOTT D. McGINNIS COLLECTION.

Snow, the perpetual enemy of transportation in northern climes, challenged operating and main-
tenance-of-way crafts. Snow battlers enjoyed only a brief respite at Montgomery when the engine
crew took water.

Frequent switch runs were necessary to shuttle cars between Lower Yard in the Minneapolis west
bank milling district and Cedar Lake, near Kenwood. PHOTOGRAPH COURTESY OF MINNEAPOLIS PUBLIC
LIBRARY, MINNEAPOLIS COLLECTION, W050.

In the fashion of the time, M&StL initially named as well as numbered its locomotives. Number 6 was called *Franklin Steele* after one of the road's early sponsors. Outshopped by Baldwin in 1877, it was assigned variously to passenger and freight duties. Here the crew takes time to pose at Albert Lea before a passenger run to Minneapolis. Note the antlers atop the headlight—not M&StL's standard operating procedure, but a jaunty exception.

American Standard locomotive 7 hurries over the open-deck trestle at Deephaven with a passenger extra, likely bearing expectant excursionists to the joys of Lake Minnetonka. Baldwin had delivered the handsome 4-4-0 in August 1877; M&StL christened her *J. S. Pillsbury*. PHOTOGRAPH COURTESY OF MINNESOTA HISTORICAL SOCIETY.

Hacks and drays on the right suggest that it is almost train time at Albert Lea's Union Depot (used by M&StL and BCR&N).

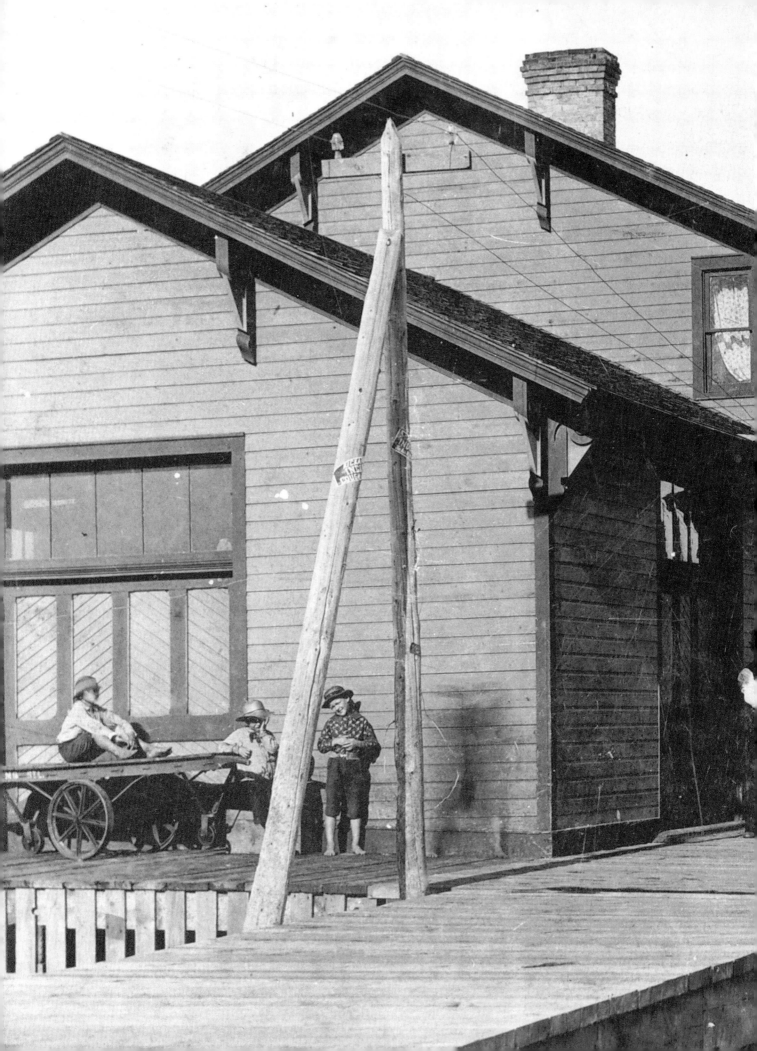

Madison, in far western Minnesota, became one of the most productive stations on the M&StL's West End. A rich volume of traffic kept the agent busy, and the demands of track maintenance in 1890 required a substantial section gang. PHOTOGRAPH COURTESY OF MINNESOTA HISTORICAL SOCIETY.

The Albert Lea roundhouse was a busy place where locomotives of both M&StL and BCR&N were serviced, turned, and made ready for the next run. All of it was labor intensive, as this view suggests.

Nasty litigation among the City of Minneapolis, Great Northern, and M&StL resulted in an expensive but ultimately very beneficial arrangement whereby the railroads lowered their grade and erected bridges for streets in the traffic-rich zone between the Mississippi River in downtown Minneapolis and Cedar Lake. M&StL likewise added yard tracks and a new freight house between Fourth and Fifth Streets. M&StL estimated the price at $150,000 to $200,000, but cost overruns doubled that amount. November 22, 1890. **PHOTOGRAPH COURTESY OF MINNEAPOLIS PUBLIC LIBRARY, MINNEAPOLIS COLLECTION.**

Waterville, about midway between Minneapolis and Albert Lea, where leased Wisconsin, Minnesota & Pacific intersected M&StL, often was a place of frenetic activity, with passengers changing trains and freight being transferred.

Aggregate demand for passenger service on the West End during the 1890s justified only one daily train in each direction between Minneapolis and Watertown. Train 13 paused daily in Madison at 9:30 a.m. en route eastward. On this day the engineer took the opportunity to oil his worthy steed.
PHOTOGRAPH BY H. MONTGOMERY. COURTESY OF MINNESOTA HISTORICAL SOCIETY.

The alley along tracks defining the metropolitan corridor at Madison in springtime was a muddy quagmire—an ornery reminder that Madison remained a raw village on the agricultural frontier. Patrons, employees, and idlers at train time on the station platform nevertheless seem undaunted.
PHOTOGRAPH BY H. MONTGOMERY. COURTESY OF MINNESOTA HISTORICAL SOCIETY.

M&StL stockholders in 1895 were told that the company owned one steam shovel but that it was "worthless except for scrap." Not surprisingly, the road in 1896 scurried around to find $2,618.66 to acquire a new one. It would find heavy duty in 1899 when M&StL worked to improve grades on the line to Albert Lea and west of Lake Minnetonka and especially in 1902–4 on Chaska Hill. SCOTT D. McGINNIS COLLECTION.

M&StL, typical of railroad companies at the time, provided outfit cars for extra gangs and bridge and building crews that moved from place to place around the system. It was a means of providing a home away from home for these hardworking employees. The foreman of this gang working near Hopkins apparently was imbued with patriotism—flying the U.S. flag over his bunk car. PHOTOGRAPH COURTESY OF MINNESOTA HISTORICAL SOCIETY.

Locomotive 40 was called for this freight extra handling a trainload of Towle's Log Cabin Maple Syrup headed for a consignee in Omaha, Nebraska—routed, most likely, via Des Moines and Chicago, Rock Island & Pacific.

On this wintry day at Waterville, locomotive 46—ironically named *Waterville* to honor that important station midway between Minneapolis and Albert Lea—has paused with train 2 at noon. In another hour it would reach Albert Lea and after a twenty-minute lunch stop would continue on down the line to Fort Dodge and Des Moines, making connections with Iowa Central at Albert Lea and Illinois Central at Fort Dodge. REX C. BEACH COLLECTION.

No matter how important the shipping base of Minneapolis was to M&StL's fortunes, business to and from small stations along the line was essential. This view from LuVerne, Iowa, was typical. In the foreground is less-than-carload freight just delivered by a drayman; at the other end of the platform is mail, express, and a hack positioned to meet the needs of arriving passengers. DENNIS HOLMES COLLECTION.

The scene was much the same down the line at Ogden, Iowa. Miscellaneous less-than-carload freight in the foreground includes oil barrels, cream cans, beer cases, and even harness racing equipment.

The arrival of train 13 at Dawson in western Minnesota on this bright day in 1898 was greeted by a huge throng of people—perhaps excursionists bound for the joys of Lake Minnetonka or the sites of Minneapolis and St. Paul or perhaps to see a newly married couple off on a honeymoon. All of it was typical during the age of railways. PHOTOGRAPH COURTESY OF MINNESOTA HISTORICAL SOCIETY.

Small wonder that photographers flocked to the tracks to memorialize that central fact of the American scene. M&StL crewmen and others took positions before locomotive 136 in this midday view (likely train 2 at Albert Lea). This 4-4-0 had come by purchase from Chicago, Rock Island & Pacific in 1905. Note the lanterns and oil cans on the walkway in front of the fireman. SCOTT D. McGINNIS COLLECTION.

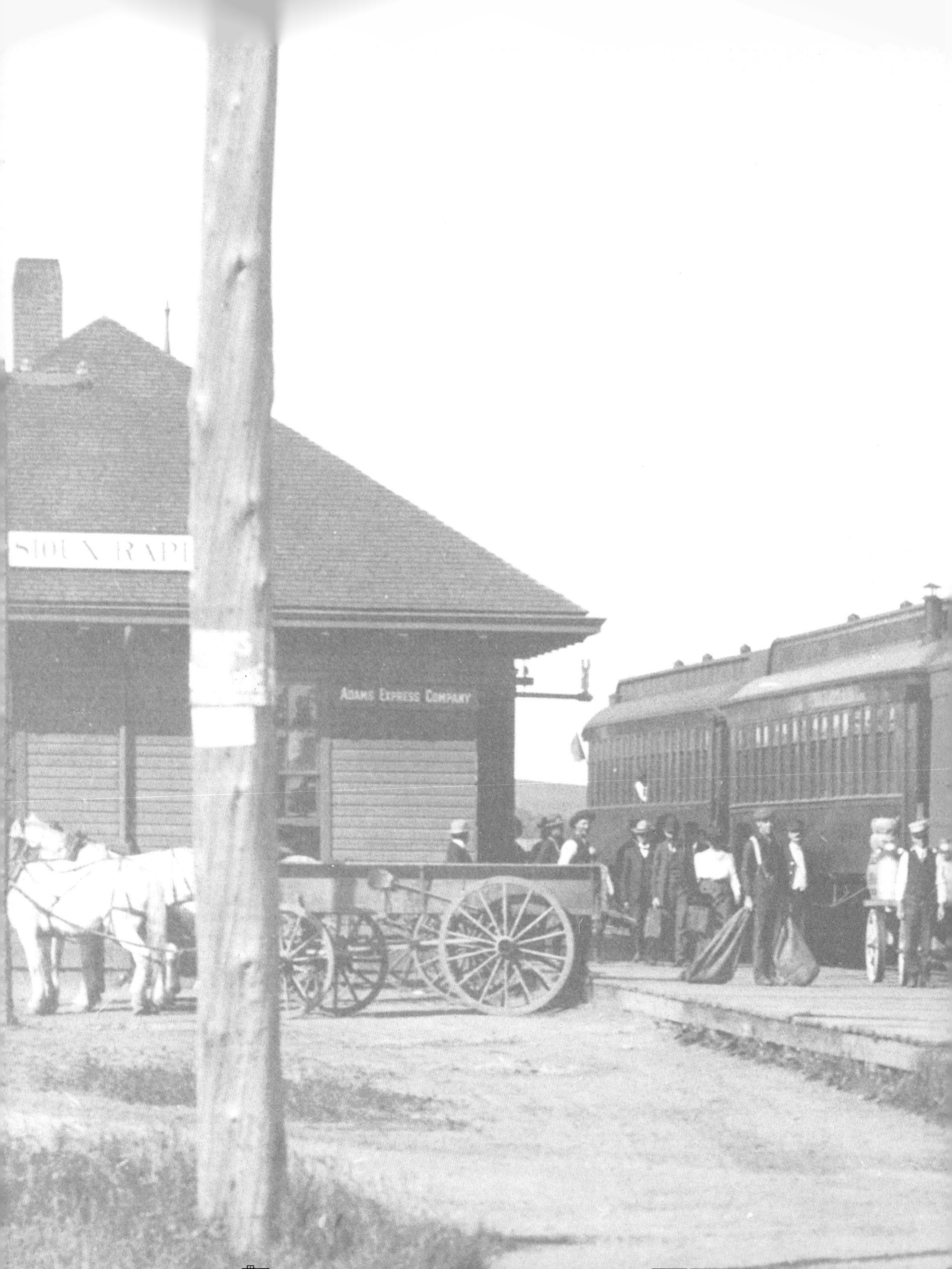
ADAMS EXPRESS COMPANY

Great Expectations

Dakota and Beyond, 1900–1923

MINNEAPOLIS & ST. LOUIS attained its ultimate reach under Edwin Hawley, who came to understand that M&StL had either to expand or to expire. But even as he planned new routes for M&StL, Hawley ended the lease of the Wisconsin, Minnesota & Pacific between Red Wing and Mankato, acquiring, however, title to its disconnected western leg between Morton, Minnesota, and Watertown, South Dakota, which M&StL had operated under lease since construction. Then Hawley began his campaign of expansion.

Residents of New Ulm, a prosperous milling and brewing community on the Minnesota River south of Winthrop on M&StL's West End, long had agitated for railroad competition (C&NW had served the place since 1872) and especially for a direct line to Minneapolis. M&StL obliged in 1895–96 through a puppet, Minneapolis, New Ulm & Southwestern, which began operation on the nineteen-mile branch on July 4, 1896. But what was implied in the word "Southwestern" in the puppet's corporate title? Hawley often was asked this question, but he remained mute until 1899, when M&StL locating engineers burst out of the Minnesota River valley at New Ulm along a course calculated to take the Hawley road to Omaha. The new line would tap the Minnesota communities of St. James and Sherburn and pass through Estherville, Spencer, and Sioux Rapids before reaching Storm Lake—all established municipalities in Iowa. Regular service commenced on August 19, 1900, over M&StL's "new Omaha extension." But M&StL never moved beyond Storm Lake, 222 miles from Minneapolis. Perhaps this was because the intervening area between Storm Lake and Omaha already was saturated with rail service, perhaps because the rougher country beyond Storm Lake would have resulted in building costs that could not be offset by local revenue, perhaps because the major roads at Omaha would have levied intolerable retaliation.

Hawley, however, was undaunted. In 1900, Hawley and friends gained control of 510-mile Iowa Central, which owned an L-shaped main line in the Hawkeye State from Northwood (just south of the Iowa–Minnesota boundary and tantalizingly close to M&StL at Albert Lea) through Mason City, Hampton, Ackley, Marshalltown, and Oskaloosa that then turned eastward, crossing the Mississippi at Keithsburg, Illinois, and pressed on through Monmouth to Peoria. In addition, Iowa Central held branches in Iowa from Oskaloosa to Albia (connecting there with Wabash Railroad for St. Louis), Hampton to Algona (crossing M&StL at Corwith), Minerva Junction to Story City, Grinnell to Montezuma, and New Sharon to Newton (with a stub to Lynnville).

Physically linking M&StL with Iowa Central to create a 488-mile thoroughfare from Minneapolis to Peoria understandably became Hawley's goal. It was complicated, involving, as it did, several roads and important strategic maneuvering among them. Iowa Central owned the line in Iowa between Manly (north of Mason City) to Northwood; Burlington, Cedar Rapids & Northern (BCR&N) had trackage rights over Iowa Central from Manly to Northwood and owned and operated the few miles between Northwood and the state line; M&StL owned but did not operate the line from the state boundary to Albert Lea; and BCR&N had trackage rights over M&StL to make the Albert Lea connection. Amid the pulling and hauling, Iowa Central gained permission from BCR&N and M&StL to run trains between Northwood and Albert Lea, in that way linking Iowa Central and M&StL for traffic purposes. That hardly ended the story. BCR&N, with prodding from powerful Chicago, Rock Island & Pacific, determined to gain an independent outlet to St. Paul and Minneapolis—putting itself in direct competition with M&StL and sundering the historic Albert Lea Route accords. For that matter, BCR&N disappeared into CRI&P's orbit in 1903. Meanwhile, another important player, Illinois Central (IC), extended a hitherto sleepy branch to Glenville, Minnesota, and with trackage rights over BCR&N/M&StL gained entry to Albert Lea. With the demise of the Albert Lea Route, Illinois Central became M&StL's partner in the Minneapolis–Chicago trade, and M&StL joined with Iowa Central and Wabash to and from St. Louis.

To properly promote and advertise these new arrangements, M&StL, on November 2, 1902, established the *North Star Limited*, a new "luxurious train" with overnight service to Chicago (via Albert Lea and Illinois Central) and St. Louis (via Albia and Wabash).

Hawley did not rest. Effective January 1, 1905, M&StL took over the lease of Des Moines & Fort Dodge (previously held by Rock Island), which duplicated M&StL in Iowa between Fort Dodge and Angus, and over which M&StL ran its trains to Des Moines. The Iowa short line also owned a line from near Fort Dodge northwestward to Ruthven. Hawley obtained trackage rights over Chicago, Milwaukee & St. Paul from that village to Spencer, thirteen miles, in that way joining M&StL's Southwestern with leased (and soon to be purchased) Des Moines & Fort Dodge. At about the same time, Iowa Central was connected to M&StL on the south by way of trackage rights over Chicago, Burlington & Quincy between Oskaloosa and Des Moines, sixty-three miles.

Minneapolis, of course, was M&StL's headquarters city and its most luscious traffic plum, especially the rich west bank milling district. The massive flour mills there had an insatiable thirst for wheat that M&StL helped satisfy. The line west to Watertown, South Dakota, increasingly was important in this regard as the wheat belt continued its shift west and north. Not surprisingly, Hawley looked in that direction; in 1906–7, work crews completed substantial expansion beyond Watertown to a fork at Conde, fifty-seven miles west, where one line stretched northwestward through Aberdeen to Leola, the other westward to the Missouri River at LeBeau. This aggregated 228 miles of new route, gave birth to sixteen communities, greatly expanded M&StL's wheat-gathering capacity, and opened an opportunity for substantial participation in the movement of cattle to and from large ranches.

Observers near and far speculated as to where Hawley would move next. Rumors were rampant. Some thought M&StL would drive all the way to the Pacific tidewater. Others, with greater merit, believed that M&StL would become an integral element in a vertical-axis transcontinental route from Canada through the American heartland to the Gulf of Mexico.

M&StL on its own held a route structure with lines serving Minnesota, Iowa, and South Dakota. Freight billings ordinarily produced three-quarters of the revenue stream; grain dominated loadings, with wheat leading. Flour in abundance moved eastward (via Peoria and M&StL/Iowa Central), and M&StL always ranked high among carriers wheeling lumber out of Minneapolis. Coal and manufactured goods added to the mix. Less-than-carload (LCL) freight proliferated; in company freight houses across the system could be found everything from caskets to corsets.

Passenger business was hardly unimportant in this age of railways, a time when railways molded the American experience and set the national tempo. Passenger trains were icons of the era. At M&StL, the proud flagship was the *North Star Limited*, actively employed in the highly competitive Minneapolis–Chicago and Minneapolis–St. Louis trade. But M&StL's overnight Minneapolis–Des Moines trains were workhorses, often double-headed, also handling cars for Omaha (via Fort Dodge and Illinois Central). Elsewhere, the *Aberdeen Limited* reigned on the new route in South Dakota. And this was a time when "hog and human," or mixed trains (handling both freight and passengers), plied branches, when commuter trains scurried from Minneapolis to Excelsior and Waconia, and when special excursion trains were routine.

M&StL's passenger trains during the Hawley years shared the St. Paul Union Depot and the Union Station at Des Moines with other roads, but much more typical for the road were humble country depots sprinkled routinely across the system. Indeed, the depot was the focal point of each community during the steamcar civilization; the depot was the funnel through which people, goods, and information passed, the prism through which country folk and small town Americans looked to the outside world. The company owned the building, true, but the depot belonged emotionally to townspeople and their rural brethren. The company's agent—the "depot agent" as he was universally labeled—was a pillar in the community, and the fact that he also was a telegrapher only gave him greater status.

Clearly there was a mystique about the depot. "Train time" always resulted in considerable milling about, hack drivers and draymen appearing as if by command, passengers heading for the platform, and the generally curious taking it all in.

Passenger trains likewise accommodated the transportation of baggage, mail, and express. On M&StL, American Express and then United States Express held the contract until it was awarded to Adams Express in 1906. En route sorting of mail by postal clerks aboard M&StL's Railway Post Office (RPO) cars began in 1882 and included car lines to Angus and Watertown; later authorizations included St. Paul & Des Moines RPO in 1886, St. Paul & Storm Lake in 1900, and both St. Paul, Watertown & Aberdeen and Conde & LeBeau in 1907 (RPO designations identified headout and terminal points).

Edwin Hawley gradually moved to fully amalgamate Iowa Central with M&StL. On December 20, 1911, the two roads merged in terms of operation although they were not combined legally until January 1, 1912. It made sense. M&StL now held a 488-mile main gut from Minneapolis to Peoria with a marvelous opportunity to expedite freight traffic through the Peoria Gateway—a route sure to please customers frustrated by awful congestion at Chicago.

And surely the merger of M&StL and Iowa Central suggested a step toward Hawley's goal of creating a north-south transcontinental. Negotiations on the north were going forward with Canadian roads, Hawley lieutenants were in the field looking to locate a line or lines between M&StL and the international boundary, and Hawley and friends held control of Missouri, Kansas & Texas (Katy), which tapped the Gulf of Mexico from St. Louis and Kansas City. All that remained, it seemed, was forging a link between M&StL and Katy. In that way the final chapter in Hawley's playbook would be executed. But whatever his plans, they were permanently shelved when Edwin Hawley died unexpectedly on February 1, 1912.

M&StL soldiered on thereafter under the leadership of Newman Erb, who bought heavier rail, ordered track segments ballasted with gravel from on-line pits, cut down grades and eased curvature, and acquired new locomotives—twelve Consolidations (2-8-0s) in 1912, fifteen Mikados (2-8-2s) in 1915, and ten 0-6-0 switchers in 1916.

Yet M&StL, as always, found itself slugging away among the titans—larger, stronger roads such as Chicago, Milwaukee & St. Paul, Chicago & North Western, and Great Northern. Fierce competition with these powerful forces was only one difficulty faced by M&StL. The West End beyond Watertown represented a burdensome legacy of debt without, as it turned out, adequate compensating revenue. The road found itself struggling to meet operating expenses and the need to service debt. Dividends, typical during the Hawley years, were suspended. In the face of all of this, Erb was still optimistic that M&StL would persevere—as long as the economy remained strong and no new unfavorable variable bubbled up.

Erb's optimism was sadly misplaced. The heavy hand of government regulation increasingly stifled managerial initiative, labor unions gained ascendancy, and motor vehicles quickly presented powerful modal competition. M&StL shuddered under the load. It was hardly alone. By late 1915, one-sixth of domestic rail mileage was in the hands of receivers, ironically, in a period of general prosperity. And fewer miles of railroad were built in 1915 than in any year since 1864.

For M&StL, confused conditions during the years of American participation in World War I only exacerbated matters. The United States Railroad Administration (USRA) took control of the country's carriers on December 28, 1917. USRA demanded that the roads terminate immigration and agricultural efforts, discontinue solicitation of traffic, trim advertising, and, instead of competing with each other, cooperate. The cumulative effect was to kill M&StL's innovative passenger program, to end through passenger service to Chicago via Albert Lea and Illinois Central, to dilute M&StL's image in the minds of the traveling public and freight customers, and, worst of all, to rob M&StL of lucrative bridge traffic moving through the Peoria Gateway. At the same time, USRA and federal legislation added significantly to railroad operating costs; rate increases to offset rising expenses did not follow. There was no surprise when M&StL's operating ratio (ratio of operating costs to operating expenses) rose alarmingly from 66.28 in 1916 to 94.73 in 1918 and to 97.61 in 1919.

Railroads finally were returned to their owners on March 1, 1920, but they had been undermaintained by USRA and thereafter remained saddled with labor costs that had mushroomed during government stewardship. In addition, a sharp postwar depression that began late in 1920 lasted until 1923, and a nasty shopmen's strike in 1922 added greatly to industry woes.

Ominous clouds appeared on M&StL's horizon. Between 1916 and 1923, operating revenues mounted by 66 percent, but operating expenses rose by nearly 100 percent. New 4-6-2s and more 2-8-2s were added to the motive power inventory, and modest improvements were made to the physical plant, but none of it was adequate to significantly improve systemwide efficiency. Against this was mirrored a mixed traffic picture. Passenger numbers tilted downward, mostly the result of vehicular competition, although freight tonnage turned upward to reflect an improving national economy. But government regulators remained obdurate in the matter of rate increases, and M&StL's bonded indebtedness and other fixed charges and debt along with taxes spelled red ink—$4.21 million of it in the three-year period 1921–23. M&StL on July 26, 1923, again found itself in receivership.

Soon after the line to New Ulm was placed in operation, M&StL established the New Ulm Switch Job, called six days per week to accomplish switching at Winthrop and station work at Lafayette, Klossner, and New Ulm. In that way M&StL could provide overnight delivery of both carload and less-than-carload freight between Minneapolis and New Ulm to the great satisfaction of customers and to the great irritation of much larger Chicago & North Western, which could not match that performance. Work done, crew and others posed for a photo at New Ulm early in the new century.

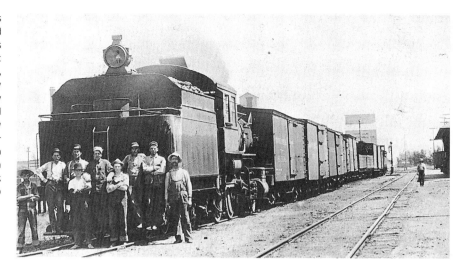

It took extensive excavation and heavy bridging to lift M&StL out of the Minnesota River valley south of New Ulm. PHOTOGRAPH BY A. J. MEYER. COURTESY OF MINNESOTA HISTORICAL SOCIETY.

M&StL had hoped to place the Southwestern in service during 1899, but weather problems and lack of rail caused delay. This construction train was found between Spencer and Cornell early in the summer of 1900.

Safely over the lengthy Little Sioux bridge, train number 14 makes a late afternoon stop at Sioux Rapids. All hands are alert to the photographer's needs.

In a scene endlessly repeated across the country during the steamcar civilization, trains met at stations large and small. Here the down freight from Winthrop is in the passing track at Monterey, Minnesota, while the up passenger train from Storm Lake, Iowa, holds the main track. In five and a half hours and after traveling 131 miles, passengers who boarded at Monterey would be in downtown Minneapolis.

The dark exhaust boiling from the stack of the yeoman 4-4-0 at the point of Iowa Central's train 3 this mild day at Union, Iowa, suggests that the fireman has responded intuitively to the engineer's demand for more steam by shoveling a few scoops of coal into the hungry firebox as the workaday local stomps out of town on its trek from Peoria to Mason City. The substantial crowd on the station platform was typical of the time. PHOTOGRAPH COURTESY OF THE UNIVERSITY OF IOWA, SPECIAL COLLECTIONS.

M&StL put its new "luxurious train," the *North Star Limited*, out for display near the Minneapolis passenger station at Washington and Fourth avenues north. A reporter for the *Minneapolis Tribune* gushed that the train's cars are "elegantly furnished throughout, the mahogany finish being particularly rich. In the buffet car is everything that a passenger might enjoy: books, magazines, stationery, and every article arranged to give the greatest convenience." The *North Star* made its initial sortie on November 2, 1902, with cars for Chicago (via Illinois Central at Albert Lea) and St. Louis (via Iowa Central at Albert Lea and Wabash at Albia). **PHOTOGRAPH COURTESY OF MINNESOTA HISTORICAL SOCIETY.**

On January 1, 1905, M&StL took lease of 138-mile Des Moines & Fort Dodge and quickly turned it into an M&StL operation. Gowrie, twenty miles southwest of Fort Dodge, was a vibrant station. Nearly out of sight in the distance is a water tank and coaling station where train 2 had paused to take on refreshment before pulling up to the platform for its daily stop at 4:59 p.m. It had departed St. Paul at 8:00 a.m. and would arrive at Des Moines Union Station at 7:25 p.m. Note the messenger toting a bag of mail to the local post office. Ca. 1910. PAUL H. STRINGHAM COLLECTION.

Des Moines & Fort Dodge in its brief and early independent life and as leased by Chicago, Rock Island & Pacific was a bare-bones operation. M&StL made improvements as it could, but the elementary and labor-intensive locomotive coaling station at Mallard spoke to a threadbare past.

The west bank flour mills had an insatiable appetite for wheat that could be partially appeased by an M&StL expansion in South Dakota. Trackage in and about the milling district was owned and operated by the Railway Transfer Company of the City of Minneapolis, a wholly-owned M&StL subsidiary. M&StL's well-respected Jerry Moynihan and his colleague R. L. Kronz stand before the 10th Avenue Yard office in 1910.

Rail went down west of Watertown beginning on August 1, 1906; crews hurried
over the inlet of Lake Kampeska and on
toward Leola and LeBeau.

M&StL's "Pacific Extension" forked at
Conde, South Dakota, 56 miles west of
Watertown, where one leg protruded
another 51 miles through Aberdeen to
Leola, and the other leg scurried 115
miles farther west to the Missouri River
at LeBeau. Conde predictably sported a
coaling station (left beyond depot) and
water tank (distant right).

Excavation became more problematic as engineers located M&StL's westward extension into the Missouri River breaks between Akaska and LeBeau.

Tracklayers followed the new grade through the rough country toward LeBeau. This segment of M&StL's Pacific extension would be thrown open to service in the late summer of 1907.

For a while M&StL operated passenger trains all the way through to Leola, South Dakota, 349 miles from St. Paul. Here in 1910 is train number 29, scheduled for a 5:50 p.m. departure from Leola on its daily-except-Sunday fourteen-hour trek to Minnesota's capital city. VAUGHN R. WARD COLLECTION.

Boosters at LeBeau fully anticipated that place to become a bustling city, especially if M&StL pushed west. In 1909, M&StL ran daily "Landseekers' Special Trains" all the way from St. Paul and Minneapolis to LeBeau "October 4 to 23, inclusive." There were great expectations, but M&StL did not move beyond the Missouri River, and LeBeau fizzled. ROBERT KOLBE COLLECTION.

Business volumes at outlying stations were brisk along M&StL lines during the age of railways. Not surprisingly, agents did what they could to secure line hauls, for which revenue did not have to be shared with other carriers, nor was it surprising that Minneapolis was the destination for much that was billed at M&StL stations. Here apples grown in the New Ulm area are loaded into an M&StL refrigerator car and dispatched to the Minneapolis market.

Grain, of course, was a mainstay of M&StL's traffic mix; wheat led. In this view from Marietta, Minnesota, in 1913, one sees grain boxes (and one carload of coal) on the house track (behind the depot) and a long string of boxes spotted on the elevator track to the right. On this fall morning, train 27, the daily rattler from Watertown to the Twin Cities, has paused briefly at 10:26 a.m. For whatever reason, a caboose has been added for this trip. COURTESY OF MADISON PUBLIC LIBRARY.

The fireman on the Ten-wheeler assigned to train 2, just arrived in Lake Mills from Albert Lea and bound for Fort Dodge and Des Moines, lounges briefly in the gangway between locomotive and tender. Soon, however, he will be hard at the business of stoking coal into a hungry firebox. Summer 1911.

Elderly and wheezy 4-4-0 number 5 often found itself during the first decade of the twentieth century assigned to commute runs out to resort stations on Lake Minnetonka west of Minneapolis.

For a while after M&StL took lease of Des Moines & Fort Dodge, it continued to run through trains from Minneapolis to Des Moines down the "Mud Line," the original route between Fort Dodge and Angus, Iowa. By 1910, however, these through passenger movements were diverted to the DM&FtD route via Tara. Passenger service on the "Mud Line" then consisted of a turn between Angus and Fort Dodge. That required a tight connection and explains why train 101 hustled northward out of Pilot Mound after a brief station stop. Ca. 1915.

En route sorting of mails was authorized early on M&StL's line down to Angus (and later Des Moines) and elsewhere as M&StL expanded and as the Post Office Department matured its sophisticated Railway Mail Service.

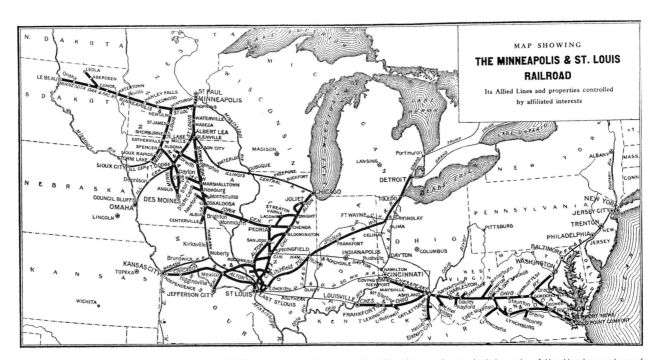

By 1909, observers of the domestic railroad scene began to take note of the Hawley system of railroads. This map shows M&StL, Iowa Central, Chicago & Alton, and Toledo, St. Louis & Western—all controlled by Hawley interests—as if they were fully integrated. They were not. Nor was Chesapeake & Ohio, another Hawley road, physically connected to the other four.

The Hook & Eye, Iowa Central's nickname, suggests informality; many observers thought that the road was also informally managed and maintained. At Manly, in 1911, the nasty derailment of an Iowa Central passenger run was caused when the leverman at the Chicago Great Western interlocker (out of sight) mistakenly threw the derailer under the train.

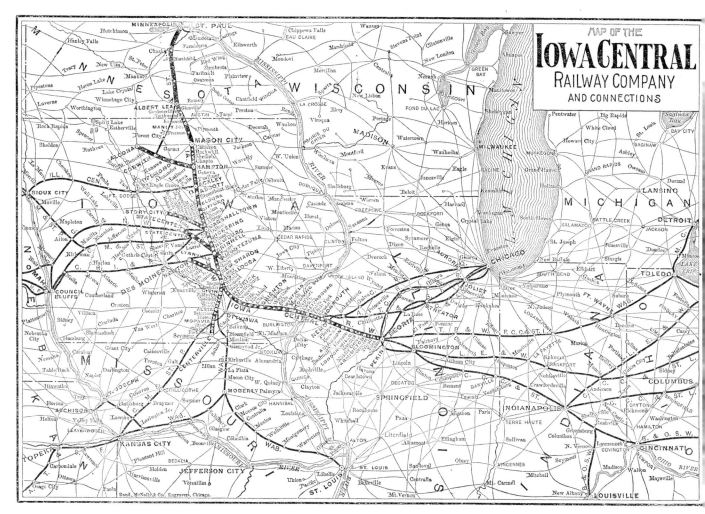

Iowa Central at its mileage apex. The
Hook & Eye was folded into M&StL on
January 1, 1912.

Iowa Central was known as a "boomer's
road," where men in the operating crafts
drifted in, worked long enough to get a
"pie card," and then left for employment
elsewhere, always, it seemed, seeking
the "big rock candy mountain." Clowning
and jocularity on the job was predictable.
DENNIS HOLMES COLLECTION.

James A. Holmes was not a boomer, but he was typical of many who went to work for Iowa Central in that he was home-grown. Born at Sheffield, he hired out at nearby Rockwell and subsequently took agency jobs at Eleanor, Illinois, and then Steamboat Rock, Iowa, where this view was made. Holmes left Iowa Central in 1909 to become a banker. DENNIS HOLMES COLLECTION.

A host of passengers and curious onlookers meet the up train from Albert Lea at the small village of Manchester, Minnesota. Ten-wheeler 205 is in charge of this day's run.

Train 2, the daytime workhorse from St. Paul to Des Moines, is about to make its daily call at Leland, Iowa, 148 miles from the Minnesota capital city and 163 miles above the Iowa capital city.

Train time at Monterey, Minnesota, on this winter day in 1905 has attracted lots of local boys as well as a collection of paying passengers, including the well-dressed drummer hurrying up the wooden platform at the left.

Workers and gawkers at Estherville, Iowa, crowd this scene, which was typical during the age of rail-ways. The drayman's wagon at left is piled high with less-than-carload freight that has come through the freight house from the boxcar on the house track in the background, every item accounted for by the agent (wearing cap with required badge and sleeve protectors); gawkers and idlers partially obscure express billings on the four-wheel cart; operator's bay at depot is on the far right.

Train time at Spencer, Iowa. The arrival of the northbound from Storm Lake about midmorning brought considerable hubbub: a large crowd, two express drays, and a hack. A mother and her brood pass by a hotel representative whose hack awaits prospective clients. At the same time the station's helper pushes an Adams Express cart to the car door; on the cart, among other items, are several cases of empty bottles headed for Schell's Brewery at New Ulm.

M&StL's depot at Echo, Minnesota, was one of several on the West End built to facilitate housing for the agent and his family.

Some of M&StL's busiest stations were on the former Iowa Central, now part and parcel of M&StL's main line. Hampton was typical of one of the larger stations and more important than many because of an important branch from there to Belmond and Algona. To the left of the southbound train is M&StL's coaling facility and standpipe; to the right is a large crowd as well as mail and express. VAUGHN R. WARD COLLECTION.

Only the dog at far right seems oblivious to the southbound passenger train or the presence of the photographer. The Eldora Railroad & Coal Company, a local enterprise, was Iowa Central's earliest predecessor. VAUGHN R. WARD COLLECTION.

Passenger, mail, and express exchanged at Searsboro, Iowa, the conductor signals "highball"—time to leave. This train is likely number 10, the maid-of-all-work between Mason City and Peoria. JAMES REUBER COLLECTION.

M&StL scheduled double-daily passenger service in both directions on several routes. This gave customers such as these about to board this southbound morning train a chance to visit or shop in nearby marketing centers. For residents of New Sharon, Iowa, the nearest larger shopping target was Oskaloosa, twelve miles distant, from whence they could make the return trip at midafternoon. VAUGHN R. WARD COLLECTION.

This view of a cluttered and unkempt depot property at Van Cleve, Iowa, may suggest that the agent was overworked or simply undermotivated. But he is wearing his cap with agent badge as M&StL required even as he loads and unloads less-than-carload freight and express on the combination car trailing the daily-except-Sunday mixed train on the State Center branch. JAMES REUBER COLLECTION.

The accoutrements of every depot office were the same: potbellied stove, wall calendars, image of a "sweet young thing," tariff cases, ticket case, captain's chair, writing tables, ticket dater, and telegraph instruments. Depot agent, telegrapher, and station helper at Madison, Minnesota, seem almost resentful of the photographer's presence in these hallowed environs. MRS. LUVERNE MEAD COLLECTION.

Idyllic country stations across M&StL's four-state service area certainly supplied impressive aggregate traffic numbers, but as a single station Minneapolis stood out. The corridor between Cedar Lake through the city to the west bank milling district was traffic rich, patrolled by switch crews.

Dawson, on M&StL's South Dakota extension in western Minnesota, boasted an unusually fine depot and an exceptionally attentive agent who created and maintained a beautifully manicured lawn and flower garden bounded by a fence that he purchased with his own resources. Beyond the depot on the left are water facilities and a coaling station; on the right is a very busy elevator track.

Edwin Hawley and then Newman Erb authorized expenditures for improvement of track structure. This included paying for extra gangs, such as this one taking a break from spreading gravel ballast on the West End between Madison and Marietta, Minnesota. But did they spend enough?

Edwin Hawley's practice in the matter of acquiring new motive power was, in a word, parsimonious. American Standard 146, resting at Monmouth, began life on Iowa Central in 1881. A new boiler extended its working years. PAUL H. STRINGHAM COLLECTION.

Twenty Mikados delivered by American Locomotive in 1915 and 1916 were immediately employed in main line duty. Typical assignments were Cedar Lake–Albert Lea, Albert Lea–Marshalltown, Marshalltown–Oskaloosa, Marshalltown–Albia, Oskaloosa–Monmouth, and Monmouth–Peoria. In some instances, an assignment began or ended in St. Paul, where 601 was lounging at the Northern Pacific engine facility, which M&StL utilized under lease.

Locomotive, caboose, and a well-manicured right-of-way near Waseca gave the appearance of
prosperity. Appearances were deceiving.

The appearance of horseless carriages before the depots at outlying villages such as *(above)* Young America, Minnesota, and *(below)* tiny Cornell, Iowa, augured only ill for M&StL and the railway industry at large. VAUGHN R. WARD COLLECTION.

The automobile immediately threatened loss of the routine business of traveling salesmen such as these dandies seen on the platform at Hanska, who might board there and go south to the next station, LaSalle, near where this three-car accommodation was photographed racing across a long pile trestle.

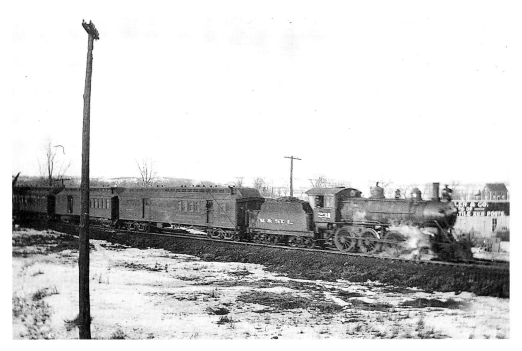

Passenger volumes predictably were heaviest on the main line; so, too, was demand for mail and express greatest there. The consist of this morning train getting away from Gifford implies as much.

As the settling and filling-in process ended across M&StL's four-state service area, there were winners and losers. Norman, Iowa, was a loser. Its depot was jacked up, loaded on flatcars, and taken a few miles to nearby Emmons, astride the Minnesota–Iowa boundary on the Albert Lea–Fort Dodge route.

Depot, Delhi, Minn.

The "metropolitan corridor" at Delhi, Minnesota, was defined by M&StL's main track and supple-
mented by house track: it was lined with grain elevators, lumberyards and coal dealers (two of each),
a stockyard as well as the railroad's depot, a windmill/water station, and a tool house. Four-car
consists on West End daylight passenger trains were typical.

Train 14 in 1915 began its daily trek to Minneapolis and St. Paul from Conde, South Dakota, making thirty-seven stops en route. Here it is hustling eastward over the Hydes Lake bridge near Young America, fifty-one miles short of its destination. Ten-wheeler 207 was received from Baldwin Loco-motive Works in 1909. PHOTOGRAPH COURTESY OF MINNESOTA HISTORICAL SOCIETY.

Switch crews in the Minneapolis milling district worked day and night in all seasons to satisfy customer needs. Notice the switchman passing signals from atop the Wabash boxcar in this cut of cars being shoved toward M&StL's yard office in the distance. October 12, 1916. PHOTOGRAPH COURTESY OF MINNESOTA HISTORICAL SOCIETY.

Snow was M&StL's perennial problem, especially on the West End and on the Southwestern. *(above)* A Mogul and an American Standard together could not defeat snow in a nasty cut three miles north of Sherburn, Minnesota, in 1912. *(below)* Shovelers finally freed the snowbound train, but a rotary plow a few days later was required to open the line.

M&StL's double-headed X-1 found tough going on the Southwestern near Searles and Hanska, Minnesota. ALFRED TIETEL COLLECTION.

M&StL rounded up its own section gangs and hired other men for snow removal. Snow lay deep in cuts as M&StL lifted out of the Des Moines River valley south of Estherville, Iowa. In this setting X-1—propelled by two locomotives with a drag-out engine trailing—has opened the line near a horse-shoe curve and waits to board shovelers who will enjoy only a brief respite from their labors. Not far ahead, just beyond Raleigh, lay Peterson's Cut, long, shallow, on a curve, and blown shut by hard-packed snow.

Snow fences were inadequate to protect Peterson's Cut, just beyond Raleigh, Iowa, to the south. Keeping the Southwestern open during the snow season was a perpetual problem. February 18, 1917.

Opening and reopening the West End in 1917 turned into a saga. Two 2-8-0s shoved the rotary plow; nevertheless, it took a full week to clear the line from Bradley to Crocker, South Dakota, a mere 7.5 miles. Twenty cases of dynamite were necessary to loosen packed snow, ice, and dirt between Wallace and Crocker. Even then the going was tough. Conde, just 17.5 miles distant, remained another seven days away. In this view X-1, with its two hard-working locomotives and a substantial train of boarding cars for shovelers, has paused in an environment that seems hardly threatening. Just ahead, however, is another long, snow-filled cut.

Aside from Minneapolis, the former Iowa Central headquarters of Marshalltown was arguably the most important place on the railroad from an operational viewpoint. In the background can be seen yards, a freight house, and engine-servicing facilities. In the immediate foreground is Chicago & North Western's vital Chicago–Council Bluffs artery and passenger station, which M&StL used under contract. The mixed train in the right foreground is likely one of the two daily turns that in 1916 worked up the thirty-eight-mile Story City branch.

Marshalltown also hosted M&StL's car shop and was home for one of the road's relief (wrecking) trains, which is in the left foreground.

The bridge and building gang, joined by the female cook and her two daughters, posed in front of the pump house at Dallas Center after rehabilitating the water system at that location. August 24, 1916.

Maintenance authorized by the United States Railroad Administration was spare, but in some cases it simply could not be avoided. This was the case at Bradley, South Dakota, when the water tank required renewal.

Numerous lengthy bridges on the Southwestern required necessary and frequent repair. Bridge 104 near Cornell, Iowa, received attention in 1917 (note the "bridge monkey," a member of the bridge and building gang, perched precariously well below the locomotive); bridge number 84 was renewed in 1919.

Some projects were beyond the capacity of company resources. Frankman Brothers contractors from Minneapolis was brought in to install the steel deck over the Skunk River on the main line at Coppock, Iowa. G. F. DOLD COLLECTION.

Necessity was the mother of invention. At hard-strapped M&StL innovation was typical. Tinkerer extraordinaire Elmer Lawrence, section foreman at Paton, Iowa, fashioned this homemade track vehicle. Lawrence, at left, has just returned from an excursion, likely unauthorized, enjoyed by his wife and others, including a large dog. Ca. 1920. JOHN B. WARTA COLLECTION.

Some days are better than others. Steam derrick (wrecker) X-3 has been summoned from Cedar Lake to pick up a derailment at Haydenville, Minnesota (between Madison and Marietta), on the West End. July 7, 1915. COURTESY OF MADISON PUBLIC LIBRARY.

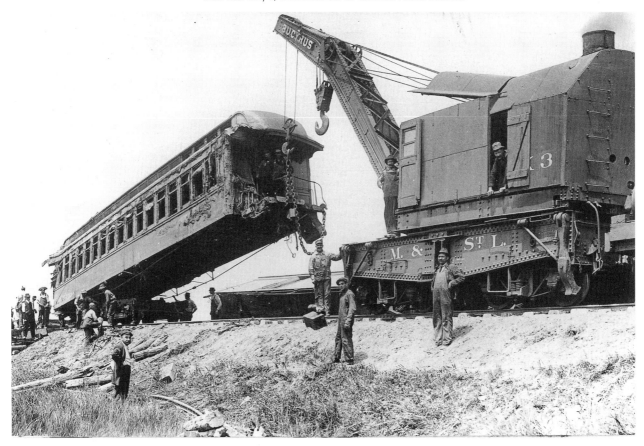

Eight persons died and thirty were injured when the locomotive tender on an upbound passenger train derailed just before a trestle over Bloody Run Creek, tumbling cars into the ravine. The rescue train from Fort Dodge has pulled up from the south. July 3, 1920.

Water was over the rail at Boyd, Minnesota, on the West End after a summer deluge during the early 1920s, but not to a depth that prevented passage of train 14 after its station stop. RPO clerks, the baggageman, and assorted passengers and crew crane to see the unexpected spectacle as the train leaves town.

Hard Times and Harder Times

Receivership—and Dismemberment?
1923–1943

MINNEAPOLIS & ST. LOUIS RAILWAY

Rᴇᴄᴇɪᴠᴇʀsʜɪᴘ ɪɴ 1923 certainly had its ironic side for Minneapolis & St. Louis. The 1920s is widely recalled as the "prosperity decade," and, indeed, in 1923—the very year M&StL slid into the courts again—the road hauled 7,311,189 tons of freight, a record to that time. But tonnage slipped thereafter, and passenger numbers, which had peaked in 1916, continued to spiral downward as the result of motor vehicle competition. The greatest problem was the company's inability to meet bonded debt coupled with a crippling recession that gripped the agricultural sector of the national economy.

The bloom clearly was off M&StL's passenger operation, although the trains still ran (most of them, at least), and railroads continued to set the tempo locally and across the land. M&StL yet advertised its *North Star* Limited ("through sleeping cars, diner, chair cars") to St. Louis (with Wabash) and connections there for New Orleans, Hot Springs, and "points in Florida and Texas." The *North Star* continued to do "very well" through 1926, but in 1927 fewer tourists headed for Minnesota resorts and fewer "commercial men" worked "the territory." Volumes were down. Demand for M&StL's train to Aberdeen, South Dakota, likewise remained strong, although in 1928 competitive bus service on the Minneapolis–Watertown leg began to erode ticket sales. The Des Moines trains were especially vulnerable to rail competition and to the increased popularity of automobiles and buses. In 1929, sleepers still plied lines to St. Louis (with Wabash), Des Moines, and Aberdeen, but the latter two were in jeopardy.

Revenue derived from hauling mail during the 1920s went up nicely, nearly tripling, and the Post Office Department maintained Railway Post Office routes on most M&StL lines although assignments on the Algona branch were trimmed back to Corwith in 1920 and ended altogether in 1922; similar service on the Story City branch terminated in 1917.

Efforts to reorganize the company, sad to say, went nowhere. M&StL posted net operating profits of $15.8 million for the decade, and the operating ratio (ratio of operating expenses to operating revenues, a common efficiency measurement among railroads) for the 1920s was a tolerable 90.42, but fixed charges resulted in a bleak net deficit of $14.7 million for the ten-year span.

Under the circumstances, senior management had few opportunities to cut down grades, ease curvature, acquire modern rolling stock, or even promote the assets of the franchise. There was no room for nostalgia. Out came the westernmost part of M&StL, twelve miles in South Dakota from Akaska to LeBeau, out came ten miles of the State Center branch in Iowa from Van Cleve to State Center, and, to raise capital and to be relieved of expensive maintenance costs, M&StL sold to Chicago, Rock Island & Pacific that portion of the main line between Albert Lea and the Iowa border (twelve miles), retaining operating rights.

On a happier note, M&StL in 1929 acquired three self-contained seventy-five-foot gas-electric cars to shoulder low-density passenger assignments. In 1930–31 came seven additional cars—these, unlike the first, did not have passenger seating but came fully equipped with thirty-foot RPO compartments plus thirty-foot baggage/express sections and were capable of toting trailing storage mail and passenger cars—plus one more self-contained car. The "GE cars," as they were called, released twenty-five lightweight and weary steam locomotives, could be operated without a fireman, proved reliable, and saved the company about $300,000 per year.

By 1930, M&StL had the cumulative experience of six decades. Its owners, managers, and employees had been tested by storms of nature, assaulted by giant railroads and more recently by vehicular competition, hammered by well-intentioned but misguided public policy, and even kicked around by dumb luck. Surely, they must have believed, they had stood up to every possible exigency. They were wrong, as the trying experience of the Great Depression soon proved.

The dark decade of the 1930s provided the country with its worst ever financial panic. Domestic manufacturing in 1932 was half of what it had been in 1929; industrial employment was down by a quarter, maybe a third. Business failures reached epidemic levels; bank suspensions added to the woe. All of this was on top of a ten-year recession that had plagued agriculture during the 1920s. Mother Nature added insult to injury across much of M&StL's four-state service area with dry, hot, and windy summers producing drought and dust bowl conditions followed by nasty winters with blizzards and bone-numbing cold. M&StL suffered right along with its constituencies—the tight symbiotic relationship of a railroad and its customer base in bold relief.

It was in this context that Minneapolis & St. Louis faced the real possibility of extinction. Several business leaders, scholars, and public policy planners argued that the country's rail net exceeded demand, especially in these depressed times and with mounting modal competition. The proper elixir for the railroad industry, they argued, was reduction in mileage to match supply with demand. M&StL became a pawn in this exercise. Powerful entities proposed that the road be dismembered: certain line segments to be acquired and operated by stronger roads, 507 miles of M&StL line to be abandoned outright, and at least 2,600 of M&StL's 3,200-person workforce to be made redundant.

Meanwhile, Lucian C. Sprague replaced William Bremner as receiver when Bremner died unexpectedly in 1934. Sprague, a "doctor of sick railroads," determined to fight dismemberment and sought the means to wiggle the road out of its dreadful financial abyss. There was no reason to expect his success.

Sprague purged the property of dilapidated motive power and rolling stock too expensive to fix or modernize, filed abandonment proceedings on several Iowa branches, and otherwise sought to stave off the coroner. Few were impressed. And the weather gods turned furious. The winter of 1935–36 was a doozy. Line segments in Iowa, Minnesota, and South Dakota were plugged routinely, cleared by weary crews and tired machinery, then shut again by new storms. Depressing gray skies, snow, and killer winds lasted for days. Trains were trapped in snow-filled cuts; much of M&StL's line from Winthrop, Minnesota, to Storm Lake, Iowa, was blocked for over a month. Digging out was slow, painful, continuous, and expensive. The ornery winter of 1935–36 finally surrendered, of course, but it proved to be one for the record books.

Even as the snows receded, the Interstate Commerce Commission handed down decisions granting most of Sprague's abandonment requests:

1. Algona–St. Benedict (8 miles)
2. Spencer–Storm Lake (37 miles, CMStP&P picking up operation of Storm Lake–Rembrandt, 12 miles)
3. Kalo Junction–Angus (44 miles)
4. Grinnell–Montezuma (14 miles)

In 1934, before Sprague arrived, M&StL had abandoned segments of the main line in southeastern Iowa but only after acquiring a "better-engineered" 30.5-mile adjacent line given up by Chicago, Burlington & Quincy from Martinsburg to Coppock. M&StL rather surprisingly also took title to CB&Q's 14.5-mile line from Oskaloosa to Tracy.

None of this was particularly interesting to those bent upon M&StL's dismemberment to provide a model in paring redundant rail net. Opposition to that plan increased, however, as affected constituencies (labor, communities that would lose service, etc.) mobilized, as Sprague campaigned for M&StL as a go-it-alone enterprise, and as he polished up the property as best he could.

The Interstate Commerce Commission would rule on dismemberment in 1938. Owners, managers, employees, and, in fact, all interested parties held their breath. Then, on June 13, good news for M&StL came from Washington: the road would not be sundered. A huge M&StL Victory Jubilee was scheduled for July 21–23 in the company's headquarters city of Minneapolis. The *Minneapolis Journal* even got up a special edition to cover the festivities.

M&StL had managed to dodge the dismemberment bullet and had reestablished itself in the minds of employees and shippers, but it still faced the knotty problem of reorganization. In the process, Sprague determined to trim more. In 1939 M&StL lopped off 6.8 miles in Iowa from the Van Cleve branch, now abbreviated as the Laurel branch, and in 1940 it abandoned everything west of Conde in South Dakota—103 miles of what some had identified as Edwin Hawley's

"Pacific" plan. In the end, by 1941 Sprague had trimmed M&StL to a system of 1,410 route miles and reduced train operation to essentials, but he had plowed money into plant and equipment and pledged to make the 488-mile main line from Minneapolis to Peoria a reliable artery adequate to attract and retain lucrative overhead traffic.

Not included as a significant part of M&StL's future was passenger operation. Bremner and then Sprague cut deeply into what once had been a rather impressive operation. The ax even fell on the road's vaunted *North Star Limited*. And M&StL exited the St. Paul passenger market.

As the 1930s ended, smiles appeared on the faces of those associated with M&StL. Even Mother Nature turned agreeable. Rains came, the dust bowl departed, and demand for agricultural produce and manufactured items increased. The Great Depression was passing; World War II was coming.

M&StL stood to gain from all of this. The Sprague plan for improvement of property and service levels continued in 1940 and beyond so that the company proved to be a willing and competent player in the railroad industry's Herculean war effort. Shopmen at Cedar Lake continued to improve the road's 2-8-2s with mechanical stokers, feedwater heaters, additional air pumps, and cross-counterbalanced main disc driving wheels. A couple of Mikados even were gussied up with stainless steel jackets; the sole-surviving Pacific, 502, was snatched from the bone yard, run through the shop, and dolled up to become the darling of the motive power fleet and Sprague's favorite stallion. Several of the newer Consolidations likewise received improvements. M&StL also took delivery of diesel-electric switch engines from four builders: Alco, Baldwin, Electro-Motive, and General Electric.

Revenue from all sources jumped as a result of the improved national economy and wartime traffic. M&StL's passenger offerings, now skeletal, nevertheless contributed to overall financial luster. Revenue from mail contracts had exceeded ticket receipts since 1932, but that pattern reversed in 1942 when rationing of rubber tires and gasoline combined with military traffic to swell passenger levels. Demand for freight transportation likewise increased dramatically, not quite doubling from 4.9 million tons in 1940 to 8.2 million tons in 1943.

Finally, on December 1, 1943—after twenty years and six months of receivership, one of the longest in history—M&StL proudly strode into the bright light of a new tomorrow. Lucian C. Sprague was elected president, M&StL stock was listed again on the New York Stock Exchange, general mortgage bonds were redeemed, and Sprague thought M&StL might be "the only Class One railroad in the country without mortgage indebtedness."

Mikado 618 has a wheel on manifest freight near St. Louis Park.

M&StL managers and directors paused for a photograph near Victoria, Minnesota, before hastening on into South Dakota for an inspection of the road's West End.

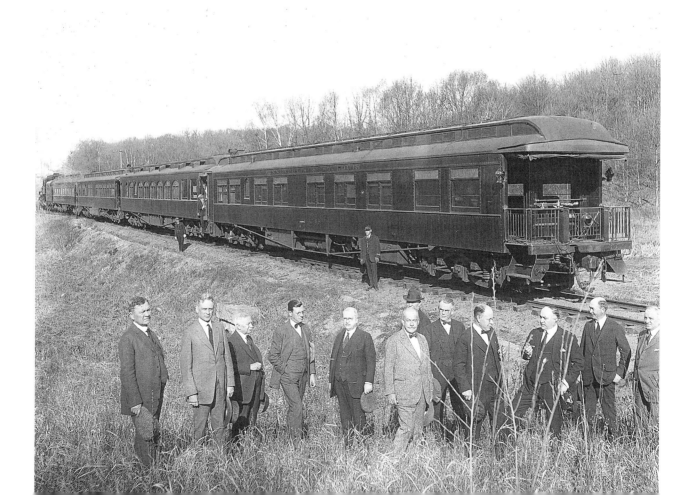

Winter frequently presented M&StL with acute operating challenges, especially on the West End. Here the road's rotary plow, X-1, plunges into a snow-filled cut near Conde, South Dakota, early in 1922. MRS. THOMAS O'DAY COLLECTION.

When the depot at Leola was destroyed by fire, M&StL's bridge and building (B&B) gang was ordered to accomplish replacement by moving the company's depot at Richmond to Leola—twenty-one miles. It took the gang three days to jack up and get supports under the depot and then get it loaded onto a flatcar. Moving day was Sunday, March 14, 1926. Given the highball signal, the train leaves Richmond. Consist: one depot and B&B equipment. JOHN B. WARTA COLLECTION.

M&StL's West End B&B gang, left to right: John B. Warta, foreman; Barbara Margan, cook; Lambert Margan; and the rest of the crew. March 13, 1926. JOHN B. WARTA COLLECTION.

Barbara Margan, cook for the West End bridge and building gang, and her daughter, Catherine, outside the front door of their rolling home. Mrs. Margan cooked for the B&B crew from 1913 until 1955, buying and preparing food wherever they happened to be. Breakfast featured bacon, eggs, pancakes, cereal, and fruit; lunch was the big meal of the day, usually meat and potatoes, vegetables, salad, bread, pie, and cookies; dinner consisted of leftovers and fried potatoes or potato salad. M&StL paid Margan's wages, but the men paid for the food: 15 cents a day in 1913, 35 cents by 1955. Morton, Minnesota, 1926.

Morton, a crew-change point on the West End between Minneapolis and Watertown, was a vibrant place. At trackside could be found the depot, hotel, engine facility, coaling platform, and grain elevators. VAUGHN R. WARD COLLECTION.

St. Paul Union Depot was a vibrant if smoky place in 1925 with a plethora of trains representing several roads coming and going at all hours of the day and night. M&StL's entry on this bright morning is second from right, likely number 13, the daily accommodation to Watertown, South Dakota, and in charge of Ten-wheeler 211. PHOTOGRAPH BY *ST. PAUL NEWS*. COURTESY OF MINNESOTA HISTORICAL SOCIETY.

Special passenger movements were no longer as frequent as they had been in the past, but on May 28, 1925, Mikado 632 headed up this impressive Shrine special at Waseca, Minnesota.

Train 16, the overnighter from Aberdeen, South Dakota, is nearly home, racing along the multitrack thoroughfare leading to St. Paul Union Depot. Near the Lafayette Street viaduct, July 23, 1925. HJELM PHOTO.

M&StL's train 2, a daylight offering, was heavily laden out of St. Paul and Minneapolis, splitting at Albert Lea, with one part heading for Marshalltown, Oskaloosa, and Albia, and the other to Fort Dodge and Des Moines.

M&StL's *North Star Limited* scorches the ballast on the double-track main line near St. Louis Park.

Morning sun shines on number 5 as it charges out of the Minnesota River bottoms between Chaska and Eden Prairie.

The West End bridge and building gang was assigned the task of salvaging rails, bridge timber, and useful ties when the line from Akaska to LeBeau was abandoned. Materials from the westward section were assembled midway and loaded by this clamshell onto empty cars shunted in by a work extra. December 1924.

The *North Star Limited* was M&StL's flagship, but its passenger offerings were more typified by maid-of-all-work trains like number 9, which loped along behind an American Standard locomotive to serve every station between Peoria and Mason City. M&StL for many years used Rock Island's passenger terminal at Peoria. July 12, 1926. **PHOTOGRAPH BY R. M. CARLSON.**

Much greater improvements to motive power, rolling stock, and physical plant might have been expected during receivership, but the court and reorganization committees proved parsimonious in the extreme. Mundane examples abound. It was a lucky section crew, such as this one at LaSalle, Minnesota *(above)*, that boasted a motor car; more typical was the handcar assigned the gang at Madison, Minnesota.

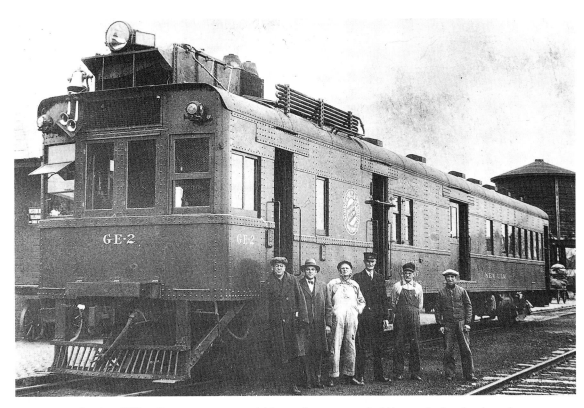

Receiver William Bremner was successful in coaxing money out of the court when he showed conclusively that acquisition of gas-electric cars for low-density passenger operation would produce net savings. GE-2, acquired in 1929, was assigned to the Winthrop–Storm Lake run, shown here at Winthrop shortly after delivery. Left to right: Walter Jaus, roundhouse foreman; Johnnie Matalowyn, traveling engineer; unidentified brakeman-baggageman; unidentified conductor; Joe Tanberg, engineer; Charles Blankenhagen, fireman.

The consist for train 2 at Mason City in April 1930 suggested that some of M&StL's passenger operation was not subject to gas-electric operation. PHOTOGRAPH BY M. B. COOKE.

Early in the Great Depression, M&StL opted to trim costs of passenger operation by acquiring gas-electric cars for all trains except its *North Star Limited*, but when train length exceeded the capacity of the cars or when the cars failed, steam would have to be summoned. That was not required on this day at Albert Lea, Minnesota. PHOTOGRAPH BY HAROLD DAVIDSON.

M&StL's motive power during the early and mid-1930s continued to resemble a museum inventory more than a stable of modern locomotives for a first-class railroad. *(above)* Mogul 311 (Mason City, summer 1935) dated from 1899; *(left)* Consolidation 463 (Fort Dodge, July 29, 1933) had been acquired by Iowa Central in 1910. *(below)* Only ten 0-6-0s, such as 82 (Cedar Lake, July 23, 1932—note landmark Kenwood water tower in the right background), plus 35 Mikados and five Pacifics could be considered modern. ABOVE PHOTOGRAPH BY WILLIAM F. ARMSTRONG; LEFT PHOTOGRAPH BY C. B. MEDIN; BELOW PHOTOGRAPH BY JOSEPH LaVELLE.

Ten-wheelers, which in another time might have been wheeling passenger trains, in the 1930s found themselves in freight service. *(above)* Lugging nineteen eastbound cars out of Marshalltown at ten miles per hour; *(below)* heading a southbound drag over the Chicago & North Western interlocker at Grand Junction, Iowa. September 27, 1935. COURTESY OF DENVER PUBLIC LIBRARY, WESTERN HISTORY COLLECTION, OTTO PERRY, OP-12784 AND OP-12783.

Mikados handled most of the manifest freight on M&StL's main line between Minneapolis and Peoria. Here 616 heads a northbound freight at Mason City, Iowa, in April 1930. PHOTOGRAPH BY M. B. COOKE.

In 1933, Reconstruction Finance Corporation's John W. Barriger III made an inspection of M&StL that included a lengthy stop at Marshalltown. Barriger was not impressed with what he saw anywhere on the property. On the right is C&NW's passenger station that M&StL shared; Barriger's special train is at left. COURTESY OF JOHN W. BARRIGER III NATIONAL RAILROAD LIBRARY.

M&StL's engine facility and yard at Mason City was a sleepy place during the mid-1930s. PHOTOGRAPH BY WILLIAM F. ARMSTRONG.

Lucian C. Sprague (right) was called to lead M&StL. Could he save it? Ten-wheeler 227 led Sprague's inspection train at Mason City on January 11, 1935. COURTESY OF MASON CITY PUBLIC LIBRARY HISTORICAL COLLECTIONS.

With Lucian C. Sprague came a few flourishes, such as striping on M&StL's locomotives. Pacific 502 sported the new look at Mason City on October 11, 1936. PHOTOGRAPH BY WILLIAM F. ARMSTRONG.

Lucian Sprague was famous for "getting out on the line." Here his special pauses at Mason City on a warm summer day in 1935. PHOTOGRAPH BY WILLIAM F. ARMSTRONG.

M&StL's daily accommodation to Watertown (left) shared St. Paul Union Depot with truly impressive trains such as Great Northern's royal *Empire Builder* (right). Could M&StL afford the rent?

Train 6, the *North Star Limited*, would
no longer race into the summer sun on
Northern Pacific's "A" line and into St.
Paul Union Depot after M&StL ended all
of its passenger service between Min-
neapolis and St. Paul on June 30, 1933.
PHOTOGRAPH BELOW COURTESY OF DENVER
PUBLIC LIBRARY, WESTERN HISTORY COLLEC-
TION, OTTO PERRY, OP-12785.

Receiver William Bremner had made the decision to exit the St. Paul passenger-carrying trade. It fell to his successor, Lucian Sprague, to pull the pin on the road's *North Star Limited*, which was first "motorized" and then simply shorn of its first-class accommodations. This was the *North Star*'s humble successor at Marshalltown on September 27, 1935. COURTESY OF DENVER PUBLIC LIBRARY, WESTERN HISTORY COLLECTION, OTTO PERRY, OP-12786.

The gods seemed everlastingly against Minneapolis & St. Louis. Bartlett Yard in Peoria, Illinois, was a bleak-looking place in 1934 when Kickapoo Creek overflowed. PHOTOGRAPH BY PAUL H. STRINGHAM.

The winter of 1935–36 was a doozy. It was bone-numbingly cold when Consolidation 400 coupled to the consist of train 57 for its run to Spencer, Iowa, from the Fort Dodge Yard. PHOTOGRAPH BY C. B. MEDIN.

Weary machines and wearier men were constantly on duty in an attempt to keep lines open. It was a hopeless task. Crews would open one route only to have it blown shut by another blizzard. Such was the case near LuVerne, Iowa, on the Albert Lea–Fort Dodge line, where Extra 400's plow was buried in snow and could not be extricated until shovelers made way for the drag-out engine to provide relief. JOHN DALLMAN COLLECTION.

A plow train became trapped on the Van Cleve branch in Iowa and was simply abandoned. PHOTOGRAPH BY WILLIAM F. ARMSTRONG.

Locomotive 458, driving a plow through packed drifts between Langdon and Terril, Iowa, broke drive rods; the badly disabled and thoroughly trapped engine blocked all attempts to clear the Southwestern. Dandies from nearby Spencer went out to mock the silent monster. No through trains operated between Winthrop and Storm Lake for more than a month.

All efforts to open the Southwestern with wedge plows failed. Hidden under a heavy blanket of snow is the plow driven by this forlorn Consolidation near Dunnell, Minnesota. But a few days later, a borrowed rotary won the battle, and soon thereafter the ornery winter of 1935–36 finally surrendered.

Bridge and building crews had their hands full with structures such as bridge 104 near Cornell, Iowa, on the Southwestern. President Sprague was determined to do everything he could to prevent dismemberment of the company. That meant dumping the high-maintenance, low-revenue segment of the Southwestern between Spencer and Storm Lake where crews often attended to needs of bridge 104.

M&StL operation at Storm Lake was on borrowed time when photographer C. B. Medin found Mogul 315 and engine crew ready for the morning run to Spencer on December 9, 1935. The last M&StL train left Storm Lake on April 25, 1936; Milwaukee Road picked up the Storm Lake–Rembrandt leg, but the rest of the line to Spencer quickly fell to the wreckers. PHOTOGRAPH BY C. B. MEDIN.

Idlers such as these fellows whiling away their time in M&StL's North Redwood waiting room were plentiful during the hard times of the 1930s. Potbellied stoves like the one in the foreground were signatures at depots around the system. PHOTOGRAPH COURTESY OF MINNESOTA HISTORICAL SOCIETY.

By the summer of 1936, M&StL's passenger offerings were skeletal. *(above)*
On most days GE-3 and its gas-electric
cousins protected the run out of Rock
Island's Peoria depot to Oskaloosa, 189
miles, but when the puddlejumpers
failed, *(right)* the company was obliged
to call out elderly cars and venerable steam engines, as was the case on
June 25, 1937. PHOTOGRAPHS BY PAUL H.
STRINGHAM.

Freight paid the bills, and if M&StL was to emerge intact from its ongoing reorganization, it needed more of it. Mikado 609 has the duty this morning in 1935 at Peoria's Bartlett Yard, likely in charge of an extra to go up Kickapoo Hill to Maxwell with a cut of westbound cars. PHOTOGRAPH BY ROBERT V. MEHLENBECK. COURTESY OF MINNESOTA TRANSPORTATION MUSEUM.

Chaska, twenty miles out from Cedar Lake Yard, always produced good freight volumes for M&StL. The Chaska Switch Job, seen here at Chaska, typically handled local work at that location and at Hopkins and Eden Prairie as well. PHOTOGRAPH BY WILLIAM F. ARMSTRONG.

M&StL's fleet of 2-8-2s provided the usual power for through freights and heavy extras between Cedar Lake and Peoria. Mikado 623 had the duty for this job crossing Willow Creek at Mason City in the fall of 1938. PHOTOGRAPH BY WILLIAM F. ARMSTRONG.

Freight volumes picked up promisingly at the end of the dark decade. Surviving locomotives from M&StL's passenger fleet—made redundant by the GE cars and by declining passenger demand—found themselves double-headed in freight service, especially between Cedar Lake and Albert Lea, and Albert Lea and Marshalltown. Pacific 503 teamed with a 600 southbound at Chaska.

Reconstruction Finance Corporation's John W. Barriger III returned to M&StL in November 1937 for another inspection. What he saw was a great improvement over earlier trips. His northbound special train paused briefly at the Oskaloosa depot. COURTESY OF JOHN W. BARRIGER III NATIONAL RAILROAD LIBRARY.

Country agents such as Joe Zigler at North Redwood noticed increased billings as demand for agricultural commodities accelerated and as weather conditions moderated. PHOTOGRAPH COURTESY OF MINNESOTA HISTORICAL SOCIETY.

By the end of the 1930s, M&StL railroaders could walk with more spring in their steps: the Great Depression was ending and their company would survive. Business picked up everywhere. Excelsior, near Lake Minnetonka on the West End, was typical. The morning local on this day has plenty of work. PHOTOGRAPH BY STUART LANE ASEY. COURTESY OF MINNESOTA TRANSPORTATION MUSEUM COLLECTION.

Increased activity in the west bank milling district of Minneapolis meant more calls for 0-6-0s.
HAROLD K. VOLLRATH COLLECTION.

Increased demand for freight transportation required more coal for company use. That was evident at Winthrop late in 1938 where several loaded hoppers were set out (right) for distribution down the Southwestern or out on the West End. The number of automobiles next to the depot and the blend of customers and employees on the platform encourage the view of recovery. COURTESY OF JOHN W. BARRIGER III NATIONAL RAILROAD LIBRARY.

M&StL fortunately boasted a bevy of talented and innovative shopmen at Cedar Lake who constantly surprised and pleased senior management with their ability to accomplish much with little. An example was Ten-wheeler 228, newly out of the shop and boldly in charge of an American Legion special departing Rock Island's Peoria passenger facility on April 10, 1938. PHOTOGRAPH BY PAUL H. STRINGHAM.

Lucian Sprague and other senior managers dreamed of acquiring modern steam power, but that did not happen. They were forced to make do with what they had—patching, painting, and then overhauling and, in some cases, making really significant improvements. That policy did not apply to the road's remaining 4-4-0s and, rather surprisingly, to M&StL's five 4-6-2s, which were consigned to the scrap heap. *(above)* Pacific 501 at Cedar Lake, and *(below)* sister 503 at Des Moines in the same season, would be written off the books in September 1939 and scrapped the next year. PHOTOGRAPH OF 503 FROM L. W. ANDREESSEN COLLECTION.

"Cedar Lake was more of a manufacturing plant than a repair shop," exclaimed a proud William L. Landmesser, who eventually became the company's master mechanic. A case in point was Consolidation 451, a favorite target for innovation, as these (below) before and (above) after scenes suggest. Among other things, 451 was given a tender booster to increase tractive effort.

Special attention was given to the road's 600s, mainstays of the main line freight fleet. Several were given Elesco superheaters, injectors, additional air pumps, and mechanical stokers, among other improvements. A gleaming stainless steel jacket was applied to 620 in 1940.

Shopmen at Cedar Lake earned a sterling reputation for innovation, resourcefulness, industriousness, and loyalty. "That shop could do anything," boasted Landmesser. "If you could not buy it they would make it." Challenges included *(left)* Mikado 606, wrecked in 1941, its forlorn elements dispatched to Cedar Lake in three gondolas and greatly in need of tender loving care. Ironically, Landmesser's father, Walter N., postponed retirement following the Japanese attack at Pearl Harbor and was on hand as lead machinist in charge of restoring the 2-8-2 to working order. *(right)* His back is to the camera, his hand signaling to the derrick operator. *(below)* The gleaming finished product emerged several weeks later to pose before the company photographer. Sad to say, 606 was wrecked again on January 31, 1942, at Searsboro, Iowa, and scrapped.

Release of modernized Mikado 611 from the Cedar Lake shop on April 8, 1941, was justification enough for this group portrait. M&StL's stable of motive power had been greatly reduced during the Depression of the 1930s; locomotives that remained would be well tested by the surge of traffic coming with an improved economy and war.

The Marshalltown car shop turned out twelve steel underframe cabooses in 1940. Three of them were presented for the photographer on September 18.

M&StL gave up on the West End in South Dakota from Conde to Akaska. The last revenue train rolled into Conde with a few cars of wheat on November 18, 1940. Scrappers soon thereafter got about their melancholy business of picking up rail and fasteners.

M&StL had dodged the dismemberment bullet, and the Sprague management team had done much to improve the physical plant, motive power fleet, and rolling stock inventory. But much work remained to be done as these views from the main line suggest—*(above)* 618 with a heavy freight at Morning Sun, Iowa, on April 28, 1940, and *(below)* 609 with another heavy load at Hanna City, Illinois, on May 22, 1940.
PHOTOGRAPH OF 609 BY PAUL B. STRINGHAM.

A booming domestic economy blended with wartime needs to put a tremendous strain on all railroads during the first half of the 1940s. Every locomotive and every car was pressed into service. On
M&StL that resulted in numerous extra movements, especially on the main line. This extra, headed
by Ten-wheeler 229 and Mikado 633 and getting a roll on tonnage out of Waterville, Minnesota, is
an example. Ca. 1942. PHOTOGRAPH BY REX C. BEACH.

Train 96 has drawn 2-8-2 engine 621
(notice the auxiliary water tank) on this
splendid fall day in 1942. The engineer
has reined in his charge, slowing for the
Rock Island crossing at appropriately
named Abbott crossing, five miles south
of Ackley, Iowa. PHOTOGRAPH BY WILLIAM F.
ARMSTRONG.

Switch jobs at Des Moines were responsible for moving cars to and from local industries, breaking up and making up trains, and making interchange with other carriers. ABOVE PHOTOGRAPH BY CHARLES E. WINTERS; BELOW PHOTOGRAPH BY WILLIAM F. ARMSTRONG.

William F. Armstrong grew up and was educated in Iowa, spending many of his early years along M&StL lines where he photographed activity. One of his favorite haunts was the 34.4-mile Story City branch that jutted westward from Minerva Junction, four miles above Marshalltown, to serve the villages of Marietta, Minerva, Clemons Grove, St. Anthony, Zearing, McCallaburg, Roland, and Story City. By 1941, service was down to a Tuesday-Thursday-Saturday mixed train that was scheduled to leave Marshalltown at 5:00 a.m. and return by 11:45 a.m. Local wags said that the train tried to get up the line in the morning and tried to return in the afternoon. Indeed, informality marked the operation. Train 341 hurrying along near Minerva Junction, about 7:00 a.m., fall 1941. PHOTOGRAPH BY WILLIAM F. ARMSTRONG.

Zearing, Iowa, about halfway up the branch, was a "good station," meaning it produced good revenue for the company. September 13, 1941. PHOTOGRAPH BY WILLIAM F. ARMSTRONG.

The Story City branch crossed Rock Island's busy Mid-Continent Line at McCallsburg, eleven miles from Story City. The crossing was protected by a gate that was opened manually and predictably set against M&StL's low-density branch. Summer 1941. PHOTOGRAPH BY WILLIAM F. ARMSTRONG.

M&StL assigned large, side-door, cupola cabooses to the Story City mixed train. Such equipment was adequate for company materials, express shipments, and the occasional passenger who happened along. McCallsburg, summer 1941. PHOTOGRAPH BY WILLIAM F. ARMSTRONG.

Roland was another good station. The depot is nearly hidden behind the caboose and short cut of cars standing on the main track while the crew attends to business on the house track. Summer 1941. PHOTOGRAPH BY WILLIAM F. ARMSTRONG.

Moguls and Ten-wheelers provided power on the Story City branch during the era of steam. On this day, a nicely polished 229 drew the honors. Story City, May 1, 1943. PHOTOGRAPH BY WILLIAM F. ARMSTRONG.

A rather substantial open-deck pile trestle was required to bridge the Skunk River near Story City. October 26, 1940. PHOTOGRAPH BY WILLIAM F. ARMSTRONG.

This view of Mogul 304 at the Roland depot does not suggest prosperity for the railroad or the town it served, but by 1941 both were doing well compared to the dreary depression of the 1930s. Fall 1941. PHOTOGRAPH BY WILLIAM F. ARMSTRONG.

Engine watered, train made up, with power, and turned on the wye at Story City, it was time to head back down the line to Marshalltown. May 1, 1943. PHOTOGRAPH BY WILLIAM F. ARMSTRONG.

A curiosity on the Newton branch was a branch from a branch—a 2.4-mile right-angle stub from Lynnville Junction to Lynnville, Iowa. In this view 2-6-0 engine 304 hustles back to the junction after a quick trip to Lynnville to pick up one loaded boxcar. November 28, 1941. PHOTOGRAPH BY WILLIAM F. ARMSTRONG.

As World War II unfolded, the Sprague team may have concluded that a mistake had been made in scrapping four of the road's five Pacifics. Heavy traffic taxed M&StL's very modest fleet of passenger steam locomotives, GE cars, and passenger rolling stock. When the GE cars failed, steam—in this case, Ten-wheeler 228—was sent to the rescue, but that put even more pressure on the tiny inventory. Waterville, Minnesota, 1942. PHOTOGRAPH BY REX C. BEACH.

Reductions in rail passenger service during World War II were an anomaly, but on March 11, 1942, M&StL terminated trains 9 and 10 between Peoria and Oskaloosa, substituting daily mixed trains and salvaging the Railway Post Office contract. The last number 9 passed Coppock at 1:15 p.m. on March 11, 1942.

A daily assignment for a Des Moines switch crew was to turn the equipment that had come in on train 4 overnight from Minneapolis and get it positioned for evening departure on train 3. VAUGHN R. WARD COLLECTION.

Let the good times roll! Handsome modernized Mikado 634 has a wheel on northbound tonnage near Mason City. September 20, 1942. PHOTOGRAPH COURTESY OF MASON CITY PUBLIC LIBRARY HISTORICAL COLLECTIONS.

The Doctor for Sick Railroads

Lucian Sprague Restores Solvency
1943–1954

MINNEAPOLIS & ST. LOUIS RAILWAY

SALAD DAYS for Minneapolis & St. Louis were few—essentially the second portion of the Sprague tenure, 1943–54. Indeed, during those years Sprague and M&StL seemed to be one and the same.

Prodigious volumes of freight necessary for the war effort and to sustain domestic needs flowed to and from stations large and small. Revenue tons for M&StL reached 1.5 billion in 1945, double that of 1938. Although the road's passenger offerings remained humble, they were absolutely essential during the transportation-short war years when gasoline and rubber tire rationing limited motor vehicle travel. In 1944, total passengers carried leapt to 262,561 (from 78,537 in 1940) and peaked at 289,372 in 1945, the highest since 1930. Operating income for the years 1943–45 was $5.9 million, net income $5.4 million, and the company paid dividends for the first time since the Hawley years.

Improvements to plant and equipment flowed as never before. New rail poured into the main line, passing tracks were extended, bridges renewed and strengthened, and ballast appeared in great abundance. M&StL in 1945 completed a lengthy program of modernizing its fleet of Mikado locomotives, the sole surviving Pacific, and selected Consolidations. Two years earlier, in 1943, the company had owned only 101 locomotives (97 fewer than a decade earlier), but these were enough to move the heavy tonnage of 1943—certainly a tribute to mechanical department personnel at Cedar Lake and elsewhere. Diesel-electric switchers had been on the property since 1938, and by now the inventory of yard goats included representatives from American Locomotive, Baldwin, General Electric, and Electro-Motive Division of General Motors. Road switchers (1,000 horse power) from Alco began arriving in 1944, and road units from EMD appeared during the next year and were quickly assigned to the 488-mile core route between Minneapolis and Peoria.

Lucian Sprague constantly sought ways to showcase M&StL. That pattern only accelerated after the end of war in August 1945. Trips to South Dakota during hunting season became a Sprague trademark. His favorite locomotive, 502, often headed special trains made up of a baggage car or two, the office car Twin Cities and cars 101 and 102, and a diner and other equipment borrowed from the larger roads at Minneapolis and St. Paul. On board were business executives, celebrities, and others whom Sprague wanted to cultivate.

Postwar prosperity held up and, not surprisingly, Sprague coaxed even more money out of M&StL's board of directors for additional improvements. Sparkling stainless steel passenger cars arrived to bob incongruously behind M&StL's venerable GE cars; new boxcars, gondolas, and hoppers entered freight service; tattered depots were replaced with new structures at several locations; and, by early 1951, M&StL rostered adequate diesel power to retire its last steam locomotives. In the same year M&StL took occupancy of its attractive new general office building at 111 East Franklin Avenue in Minneapolis. M&StL was no longer "Miserable & Still Limping," beamed Lucian Sprague; rather, it was "Modern & Streamlined."

Sprague was fully at the throttle. "All's well with M&StL," declared Newsweek for December 18, 1950. Shippers and railroad managers elsewhere noted with admiration M&StL's efficiency over the Peoria Gateway, and financial circles pointed approvingly to the company's lack of bonded indebtedness. The road's stock had traded as high as $93 per share prior to a four-for-one split in 1946, and it ranged from $11 to $28 thereafter, trending generally upward.

All seemed well at M&StL, but, in fact, storm clouds were forming over it and over the entire railroad industry. Competitive assault came from several sources, especially motor vehicles. Trucks ran off with increasing chunks of highly rated freight and even grain and livestock. Automobiles claimed an accelerating portion of intercity passenger miles, and airplanes skimmed off long-distance travelers. In 1954, American Airlines handled more passengers than any single railroad. Railroads' share of intercity freight volume was down to just over 50 percent; truckers, pipelines, and inland waterways split the remainder in nearly equal portions. Wall Street analysts and other observers were increasingly pessimistic about the railroad industry. But if Lucian C. Sprague had any qualms about the industry or about M&StL in particular, he certainly did not show it.

Sprague's dramatic rescue of M&StL remained deeply embedded in railroad lore. If ever there was a silk purse made from a sow's ear, it was M&StL. Raiders took note. Indeed, led by Ben W. Heineman of Chicago, they ousted Sprague through a bitter proxy battle in 1954. A new director promised a new management team and a new direction for M&StL. Loyal employees and patrons wondered if the world had been turned upside down.

Bartlett Yard, at the easternmost edge of M&StL's domain, received and dispatched tonnage to and from M&StL's multiple interchange partners at Peoria. PHOTOGRAPH BY HENRY J. MCCORD.

M&StL's passenger operations during World War II reflected national patterns: trains were jammed. But M&StL's contribution was slim compared to others that shared Great Northern's spacious passenger terminal at Minneapolis. Here GE-31 is about to depart with train 2, a daily-except-Sunday Albert Lea turn.

Train 18 is well off the advertised as it paused this day at New Ulm, but engineer Jack Whitman from Fort Dodge seems unapologetic as he leans out the cab window of GE-2. With baggage, mail, express, and a few hearty passengers aboard, Whitman's charge will assault a lengthy grade taking M&StL from the clutches of the Minnesota and Cottonwood river valleys southward to Searles and beyond.

M&StL during the 1930s pared its motive power roster to the bone, but with the press of war traffic even old mills such as Consolidation 445 found great utility. On this day 445 had the switching duty at Albert Lea. PHOTOGRAPH BY HAROLD DAVIDSON.

World War II resulted in massive scrap drives including the dismantling of 121 miles of original over-land route trackage in Utah. Southern Pacific arranged for appropriate "unspiking" ceremonies at Promontory Summit on September 8, 1942. Two diminutive locomotives owned by Hyman-Michaels Company, the dismantler, faced each other mocking the scene from May 10, 1869, when the trans-continental route was finished at that location. Ironically, the two locomotives assigned in 1942 were ex-M&StL 311 and 319, 2-6-0s that the Sprague management had seen as surplus and then sold to Hyman-Michaels, showing up at Promontory in roles unimagined.

Thrice weekly, M&StL dispatched mixed trains to Leola, South Dakota, from Aberdeen. Saturdays were particularly busy at Leola where livestock in substantial number was loaded out by area cattlemen. Animals typically were consigned to South St. Paul or to Chicago Union Stockyards.

It was dirt-track railroad for the most part west of Watertown, South Dakota, but section gangs such as this one at Nahon, between Aberdeen and Stratford, took pride in a well-groomed property.

Throughout the war years, M&StL operated daily-except-Sunday mixed-train service between Watertown and Aberdeen. Passengers were scarce in the elderly combine that bobbed along behind a string of freight cars, but dispatchers kept the trains on schedule as best they could to protect the Railway Post Office authorization. The James River was in flood near Stratford (milepost 308) when this view of Train 115 was made in April 1943.

Occasionally work bunched up and M&StL was obliged to call out an extra on the Story City branch.
On this day trip 4-6-0 engine 229 had the honors—steaming proudly through Zearling, twenty-two
miles from Marshalltown and sixteen miles from Story City. PHOTOGRAPH BY WILLIAM F. ARMSTRONG.

A stiff grade up Kickapoo Hill from Bartlett Yard in Peoria to Maxwell, not quite five miles, presented operational challenges. On this day in 1942, *(above)* two 600s (2-8-2s) on the point and *(below)* one stout (booster-equipped) 400 (2-8-0) were required to wrestle westbound tonnage out of the stubborn Illinois River valley. **PHOTOGRAPHS BY DAVID LEWIS.**

Helpers on westbound freights out of Bartlett Yard were routine. Mikado 621 helped train 9 up to Maxwell, where the crew took time to pose for the photographer on May 6, 1944. PHOTOGRAPH BY DAVID LEWIS.

Train 395, shown here entering Oskaloosa, handled Wabash tonnage from Albia. Those cars were added to tonnage arriving from Peoria and then moved on to Marshalltown, Albert Lea, and Cedar Lake as train 95—one of M&StL's few time freights. 1944. FRED JACKSON COLLECTION.

Dropping tonnage downgrade from Maxwell to Peoria presented its own problems. The lead locomotive on this eastbound coal train has already shut off, and the road locomotive following will do so shortly. Enginemen had better know how to "work the air," lest they risk a runaway. May 6, 1944.
PHOTOGRAPH BY DAVID LEWIS.

Chronically short of power during the war years and faced with an unforgiving profile across much of its main line between Minneapolis and Peoria, M&StL often resorted to double-heading freights. A frequent scene out of Cedar Lake to Albert Lea was Pacific 502 leading one of the road's modernized 2-8-2s. *(above)* The earth shook as 502, coupled with 621, pounded over H&D crossing (CMStP&P, west of Hopkins) with heavy eastbound tonnage early in the war years and *(below)* rolled southbound near New Prague.

It fell to M&StL's fleet of improved 2-8-2s to handle the bulk of main line tonnage during the war. They performed beautifully.
(above) Assaulting Chaska Hill between Chaska and Eden Prairie. *(right)* A southbound extra with a light train near Carver.
(left) Almost home, a northbound extra in 1945 passes through Eden Prairie, twelve miles from Cedar Lake Yard outside of
Minneapolis.

Cedar Lake was the site of M&StL's primary Minneapolis yard as well as its principal engine terminal and shop facility. BELOW PHOTOGRAPH BY WILLIAM F. ARMSTRONG.

M&StL's Middle Yard in Minneapolis was dense with cars moving to or from team tracks, industrial spots, loading/unloading facilities, and freight houses.

M&StL had long experience with gas-electric cars and recently had acquired diesel-electric switchers when Electro-Motive Division of General Motors showcased its new FT freighters. M&StL hosted two of the FTs on a trial run from Cedar Lake to Mason City, Iowa, in February 1939. Onlookers at Mason City must have wondered what they beheld. PHOTOGRAPH BY WILLIAM F. ARMSTRONG.

To differentiate between its steam roster and newly arrived diesels, M&StL initially placed a "D" in front of the road number, which was itself a curiosity because the road number was determined by the month and year that the unit arrived on the property. Thus D-939 identified this Alco product as one that M&StL acquired in September 1939; it saw long service at Cedar Lake. PHOTOGRAPH BY JAMES G. LaVAKE.

M&StL found in Alco RS-1s exactly what it wanted: gritty units that could be assigned variously to yard duty, road work, and even passenger operation. The first, 244, arrived early in 1944. Its sister, 944, posed behind Lucian C. Sprague and other officers seated in a Stanley Steamer at Cedar Lake on October 25, 1944.

In October 1944, M&StL began bargaining with Electro-Motive to acquire two three-unit FTs for main line freight service. The second of these, 545, arrived on May 5, 1945, was polished up and put on display at the Parade Grounds near Cedar Lake. Retired locomotive engineer George Nelson must have marveled at the shiny new steed.

Lucian Sprague's favorite stallion was Pacific 502, which Cedar Lake shopmen gussied up and improved, much to Sprague's delight. The attractive 4-6-2 saw yeoman duty in freight service during the war and could be counted on to head special passenger movements such as directors' specials and the like. These became more frequent after the war as Sprague sought to advertise the road among shippers, public authorities, and friends of the road. Minneapolis, September 28, 1945.

Cedar Lake was home to M&StL's dispatchers, a thoroughly competent crew. 1951. *Left to right:* E. E. Sperry (chief), James E. Dwyer, Manford J. Reitan (night chief), George R. Cook, W. C. Filbrandt, Martin Lothringer, Roger Button, Ole Wiberg, O. M. Olson, and Archie Vaughn; seated behind: Roy N. Perkins; seated in front: E. L. Callies. **MANFORD J. REITAN COLLECTION.**

Marshalltown was an important location on M&StL, with car shops, engine facility, and a substantial yard. November 9, 1947. PHOTOGRAPH BY DON CHRISTENSEN.

Fort Dodge, Iowa, was home terminal for crews handling freight assignments to Des Moines, Estherville, and Albert Lea. Normal power for such runs were 2-8-0s such as 454 seen at the engine facility on August 10, 1946. **PHOTOGRAPH BY JOSEPH LaVELLE.**

Train 50 was the daily-except-Sunday freight on the Albert Lea–Fort Dodge leg, doing local work en route and also handling important interchange traffic for Illinois Central at Fort Dodge—the likely destination for the block of refrigerator cars trailing the two head cars on this train at Corwith on June 21, 1946. Train 50, and its counterpart train 51, took coal and water at Corwith and also picked up and set out tonnage to and from the St. Benedict branch. **PHOTOGRAPH BY WILLIAM F. ARMSTRONG.**

Monmouth, Illinois, was the intermediate terminal between Oskaloosa and Peoria. Crews were changed there and locomotives were changed and serviced. Mikado 629 even gets a squirt of oil for the locomotive's bell. PHOTOGRAPH BY WILLIAM F. ARMSTRONG.

After devastating floods in 1947 took out M&StL's (formerly CB&Q's) bridge near Tracy, Iowa, traffic between Oskaloosa and Des Moines was routed via Albia and trackage rights over Wabash/CB&Q to and from Iowa's capital city. On this day in April 1948 traffic demanded a double-headed extra from Des Moines, shown here hustling into Oskaloosa with heavy tonnage, much of it likely destined for Peoria and beyond. PHOTOGRAPH BY ROBERT H. MILNER.

The photographer was captivated by M&StL's Iowa branches. On this day in April 1946, the dispatcher has annulled train 342 and engine 304 will run extra from Minerva Junction (where a proud engineer paused before his steed) to Marshalltown. PHOTOGRAPH BY WILLIAM F. ARMSTRONG.

Spritely Ten-wheeler 226 drew the assignment for this extra headed west between McCallsburg and Roland, Iowa, on February 24, 1947. PHOTOGRAPH BY WILLIAM F. ARMSTRONG.

Train 390 picked up an empty gondola at Denhart, Iowa. PHOTOGRAPH BY WILLIAM F. ARMSTRONG.

Kanawha, Iowa, was an obligatory station stop. Note the two tykes, now weary of activity at the depot and scurrying away toward town. PHOTOGRAPH BY WILLIAM F. ARMSTRONG.

Belmond was an important station on the Corwith branch, but such importance was not evident from M&StL's weary-looking depot and decrepit water tank. Grain door boards stacked up at left are a better gauge of Belmond's importance to the railroad. PHOTOGRAPH BY WILLIAM F. ARMSTRONG.

Extra 620 East roaring over the Milwaukee crossing near Hopkins oozed postwar confidence at M&StL.

Coal from substantial pits at Rapatee and Middle Grove, Illinois, moved routinely to interchange at Peoria. Bartlett Yard, February 14, 1947. PHOTOGRAPH BY PAUL H. STRINGHAM.

Train 95 with 456 and 620 coupled is late this morning in 1947 as it heads toward Hopkins and on to Cedar Lake Yard where road power will be cut off and a new locomotive assigned to hustle some of the consist to Minnesota Transfer and other interchange at St. Paul. PHOTOGRAPHS BY JAMES G. LaVAKE.

Two 600s, pinch-hitting for diesels normally assigned to time freight 20, pick their way through the scene of a nasty accident near Jordon late in July 1947.

Consolidation 456 was embarrassed in February 1948 two miles north of Ormsby, Minnesota, on the Southwestern when it and plow X-587 were derailed trying to open a long shallow cut. It was nearly the last gasp of steam on that part of M&StL. PHOTOGRAPH BY VIRGIL W. PETERSON.

Steam and diesel mixed in road service (H&D crossing between Hopkins and Eden Prairie).

Pacific 502, Lucian Sprague's favorite, took a bow at the 1949 Chicago Railroad Fair and then, sad to say, headed for the scrap yard. PHOTOGRAPH BY C. B. MEDIN.

Time freight 20 arrives in Oskaloosa's North Yard; 0-6-0 engine 87 hurries to work the train. At right are M&StL stock cars.

The view from the fireman's side of brand-new EMD F-7 two-unit 150 eastbound at Olds, Iowa, in February 1950. The venerable coal chute and water supply soon will disappear, the need for them gone with the demise of steam power. PHOTOGRAPH BY ROBERT H. MILNER.

Extra 310 off the Newton branch drifts into Oskaloosa at dusk behind a Schenectady-built 2-6-0 of 1899 vintage. The final call for steam at M&StL might have been for such an unremarked old mill. July 28, 1950. PHOTOGRAPH BY ROBERT H. MILNER.

Mail revenues increasingly were important to M&StL passenger fortunes.
(below) Train 14 (from Watertown) at
Deephaven and *(far right below)* train 7
(from Albia) at Mason City. NEAR RIGHT
PHOTOGRAPH BY GORDON E. LLOYD.

GRINNELL COLLEGE
Department of Latin
GRINNELL, IOWA

Mr. John F. Bridgham
188 Parker Ave.
Benton Harbor
Mich.

GE-27 and trailing equipment arrived in Des Moines with train 4 from Minneapolis at 7:30 a.m. and have been turned to await departure as train 3 (generally right behind Rock Island's westbound *Rocky Mountain Rocket*) at 8:00 p.m. M&StL's varnish was old and out of fashion. PHOTOGRAPH BY DON CHRISTENSEN.

In 1948, M&StL proudly took delivery of six stainless steel coaches that were deployed on passenger trains to Watertown, Albert Lea, Albia, and Des Moines. On one of the first trips with the new equipment, train 7 paused before the handsome depot at Oskaloosa. May 30, 1948.

When the Budd coaches arrived in 1948, M&StL operated trains 1 and 2 on daylight schedules opposite night trains 3 and 4 on the Minneapolis–Albert Lea segment. Soon, however, trains 1 and 2 were given daylight runs all the way to Fort Dodge and Des Moines, and trains 3 and 4 were removed from timetables. Here is train 2 clattering over the Milwaukee Road diamond at Chaska, Minnesota.

Mail and express at Albert Lea for train 2, down from Minneapolis en route to Fort Dodge and Des Moines, was heavy.

EMD delivered two-unit F3 locomotives, such as 348, that were deployed in general service on the main line and on the West End to Watertown. On this day in 1948 nearly new 348 is wheeling tonnage from Morton on an extra assignment that soon will enter the main line at Hopkins.

M&StL ultimately rostered three General Electric 44-tonners, normally deployed to switching assignments at Mason City and Fort Dodge, but they were not strangers on some of the Iowa branches. *(right)* D-742 at Mason City; *(below)* 149 at Roland on the Story City branch. 1950.
PHOTOGRAPHS BY WILLIAM F. ARMSTRONG.

D-842 on April 14, 1946, found itself assigned to the daylight switch job at Fort Dodge, shown here spotting cars at the Cargill plant. PHOTOGRAPH BY EDWARD WILKOMMEN.

Alcos often found themselves on work train duty. *(above)* Here are engine 244 on flood duty at Carver (bridge 22) in May 1949, *(below)* 244 on a steel gang at Winthrop in the fall of 1949, and *(right)* 546 on a weed spray train at Spencer, June 1950.

If Alcos had a typical assignment at
M&StL, it was in local freight service.
(above) Train 10 performing switch
duties at Abingdon, Illinois, May 22, 1949.
(below) Train 10 in the yard at Monmouth,
Illinois, September 8, 1952. PHOTOGRAPH
BY GORDON E. LLOYD.

Frank Donovan's *Mileposts on the Prairie* and M&StL were on prominent display at Powers Department Store in downtown Minneapolis, February 1951.

Frank Donovan in *Mileposts on the Prairie* portrayed M&StL as a hard-luck road that had overcome great odds to become an important player in its four-state service area. Donovan could point with pride to *(left)* M&StL's tidy diesel shop at Cedar Lake; *(below)* M&StL's increasingly popular time freight 20 (in this view drifting into Oskaloosa), and *(above)* M&StL's shiny stainless steel passenger coaches (train 2, Fort Dodge). ABOVE PHOTOGRAPH BY BASIL W. KOOB. BELOW PHOTOGRAPH BY ROBERT H. MILNER.

Wrecks on M&StL were infrequent, but hardly unknown. On July 21, 1947, Extra 147 rear-ended train 20, disturbing an otherwise idyllic rural scene near Jordan, Minnesota. Wrecking derricks and crews from Cedar Lake and Marshalltown were required to put things right.

Lucian C. Sprague, "doctor for sick railroads."

Alco 944 and caboose became trapped near Bradley, South Dakota, in February 1946. It took four days and valiant efforts by Work Extra 1144, plus one helper and a drag-out engine along with support personnel, to open the line. In one case, two Alcos attacked a cut at perhaps 40 miles per hour, with little success. A "snoose"-chewing conductor riding in the second Alco spit into the snowbank after each attempt—measuring meager progress, about eight inches, each time.

Nasty storms hit the West End again late in 1952. In South Dakota a Russell plow, three Alcos, a cook car, and three cabooses (to provide board and room for train and engine crews in that thinly populated part of M&StL's domain) were required to clear the lines.

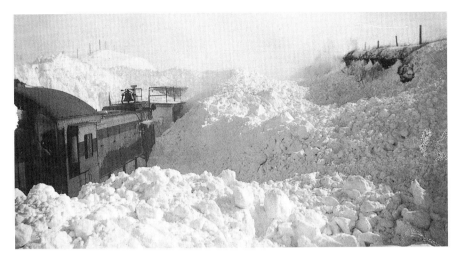

Long, deep cuts between Crandall and Crocker, South Dakota, presented problems every snow season. It was a difficult chore for Russell plows and hearty Alcos, especially when the Russell lifted off the rails and careened toward the right-of-way fence.

(below) The engineer's view of Ackley, Iowa, coming from the south. Ahead is M&StL's depot "built for the ages" and tenderly cared for by an attentive agent, Dan N. Knight.

Early each evening a switcher delivered the consist for train 13 to Great Northern's station in downtown Minneapolis. Mail, express, baggage, and then passengers were loaded for an 8:00 p.m. departure for Watertown and points en route. 1952. PHOTOGRAPH BY JAMES G. LaVAKE.

M&StL's earliest corporate predecessor was the Eldora-based Eldora Railroad & Coal Company. Train 7 made a daily stop at that historic location. It was a scene etched indelibly on the country's landscape even in the early 1950s. On this bright morning the conductor wishes a word with the engineer before heading on to Albert Lea and all stations en route.

Special passenger movements in the 1950s were rare but not unheard of. On May 20, 1953, M&StL handled the annual Des Moines Goodwill (Chamber of Commerce) train from Estherville to Des Moines. Alco 446 and heater car 501 caught the assignment of wheeling six heavyweight Pullmans and their ebullient ambassadors. Spencer, Iowa.

Freight paid most of the bills, and M&StL focused on generating tonnage over its main line. Oskaloosa's North Yard reflected as much. On this afternoon view from July 28, 1950, flagship train 20 (at far left) is moving out of town for its daily sprint to Peoria while train 95 behind engine 448 heads toward its eventual Twin Cities destination. To the right is the caboose and consist for train 396, assorted rolling stock, and company facilities. PHOTOGRAPH BY ROBERT H. MILNER.

Train 396 passes over Chicago, Rock Island & Pacific as it departs Oskaloosa "on time" (3:50 p.m.) for Albia and Des Moines. July 28, 1950.
PHOTOGRAPH BY ROBERT H. MILNER.

Switching was as unromantic as it was essential. Crews such as this one at Cedar Lake in the summer of 1952 made up and broke up trains as a regular twenty-four hour routine. PHOTOGRAPH BY JAMES G. LaVAKE.

Caboose hops such as this one at Minneapolis in the summer of 1952 were routine in moving interchange cars to and from Cedar Lake and Minnesota Transfer. In this case, however, power and caboose were heading over to St. Paul to pick up number 96's train. PHOTOGRAPH BY JAMES G. LaVAKE.

During the early 1950s, M&StL often employed a single F unit to power trains 74 and 75, daily-except-Sunday local freights between Morton, Minnesota, and Watertown, South Dakota. Saturdays typically produced substantial livestock movements on the West End. *(left)* Note the stock cars behind the empty flat of train 74 at Dawson, Minnesota, Saturday, April 22, 1950. *(below)* Train 74 whizzes through Boyd, Minnesota, in May 1950. **PHOTOGRAPHS BY ERNEST LEHMANN.**

The engine crew of Extra 350 East had a clear view as they headed over the Mississippi River bridge at Keithsburg, Illinois, but they had every good reason to wonder where the company that employed them was headed.

M&StL's handsome new diesel shop at Marshalltown lent credence to Sprague's assertion that M&StL stood for "Modern & Streamlined."

A Fresh Approach?

The Minneapolis & St. Louis Railway
Adjusts to "Modern Management"
1954–1960

MINNEAPOLIS & ST. LOUIS RAILWAY

Bᴇɴ ᴡ. ʜᴇɪɴᴇᴍᴀɴ admitted that he was no railroader and said he had "no spectacular plans" for M&StL, but he promised that he would take a "long, careful" look at the company. Sprague was out and so were a few of his lieutenants. John W. Devins, long in employ at M&StL, was named president yet proved to be little more than window dressing and soon was gone, as were many other longtime managers. In were a group of young lions led by Albert W. Schroeder and supported by Larry S. Provo, among others.

The new team proved as aggressive as it was innovative. Sprague had made much of M&StL's ability to expedite tonnage via the Peoria Gateway—taking cars from the west delivered primarily by Great Northern and Northern Pacific to Minneapolis, let's say, and whisking them to Peoria in about sixteen hours, holding M&StL's per diem liability on those cars to a single day and putting broad smiles on the faces of shippers who congratulated themselves on saving the anguish of great delay if routed through heavily congested Chicago. Schroeder and company built on that legacy by significant betterments to the road's 488-mile Cedar Lake–Bartlett yard corridor. But they took clear aim at what they considered M&StL's antiquated or curious practices. Provo, for example, replaced manual accounting procedures—and those employees engaged in them—with efficient new IBM equipment. Small wonder that Provo was seen as "the agent of curtailment."

On another front, M&StL's new management shook their heads at the road's curious system of numbering diesel locomotives to correspond (roughly) with the month and year of receipt. Alco 244, M&StL's first RS1, for instance, had arrived in February 1944. Presently it became 200; all other Alcos were renumbered in sequential order. Switchers took lower numbers in single digits or in 100 series; two SD7s became 300 and 301; the EMD F3s and F7s became 400s and the FTS 500s. It made sense. Far less justified was the decision to knock out the ampersand in M&StL and to usher in a new "MStL" logo. And the decision to embrace a new color scheme—fire engine red and off-white—simply to align M&StL's colors with those of Schroeder's alma mater, the University of Nebraska (a state not touched by M&StL), was nonsense.

Ironically, Heineman's successful proxy war against Sprague in 1954 came just as the country's rail industry was faltering. In 1953 railroads handled 53 percent of domestic ton miles, down from 63 percent in 1939. Freight revenues in 1954 were $7.8 billion, about what they had been in 1948; net income, however, was $683 million, essentially that of 1946. This, managers and investors moaned in unison, was after railroads had spent lavishly to modernize plant, motive power, and rolling stock. The railroad industry was in trouble; its rate of return on investment in 1954 was a mere 3 percent.

Schroeder and crew at M&StL were hardly unaffected. They were obliged to demand a leaner operation while at the same time trying to hold traditional customers and attract new ones against expanding and often publicly subsidized modal competition. Little could be done to trim branches (that task had been accomplished early in the Sprague years); Schroeder focused on reducing employee numbers—extending the jurisdictions of section gangs, mechanizing track work, and closing or dualizing rural stations.

Not surprisingly, Schroeder's "sharp pencil" group turned steely eyes to M&StL's highly abbreviated passenger operation. The road sold its six Budd stainless steel coaches, rebuilt four venerable GE cars in order to shoehorn accommodation for passengers into the tiny hind section of the cars, and bought a couple of RDC4s from Budd to be placed on the Minneapolis–Des Moines assignment. The modified GE cars worked the Albert Lea–Albia and Minneapolis–Watertown jobs. Mail volume to Des Moines required that the RDCs tow a trailer, but they had not been designed for such strenuous duty, and on M&StL they proved inadequate.

All of this was backdrop to declining passenger numbers. The ax first fell on trains 7 and 8 working the main line between Albia and Albert Lea; the last runs occurred with little fanfare on May 31, 1958. Trains 3 and 4 on the longer Minneapolis–Albert Lea and Fort Dodge–Des Moines assignment perished on March 21, 1959 (trains for mail service only continued until April 19). That left only the Watertown run, trains 13 and 14, essentially mail trains, although an unkind observer might have labeled them mixed trains for they handled not only passengers, mail, and express but also less-than-carload freight and occasionally carload freight, such as potatoes from Watertown or dairy products from Clarkfield. The last miles were run off on July 21, 1960.

Meanwhile, early in 1956 Ben Heineman made his departure from the active affairs of M&StL following a successful if uninvited proxy contest for control of woe-enwrapped Chicago & North Western. The ramifications for M&StL were not immediately apparent.

Heineman's absence from M&StL coincided with deepening problems for the country's rail industry, including M&StL. Traffic solicitors confronted a constant need to put freight over M&StL lines in an environment that was ever more competitive, always fluid, and subject to weather conditions affecting crops, vacillating government agricultural policy, strikes in major industries, the traditional ebb and flow in the building trades and construction industry, and vicissitudes of the business cycle. During the first half of the 1950s, M&StL saw 54.6 percent of its tonnage interchanged to or from connections. This dependency on the goodwill of others threw into bold relief M&StL's historic problem of short average hauls and raised again the perennial question of how the road might lengthen carries. The era of expanding system through construction long since was over, but a merger was a tempting alternative.

Before he left for C&NW, Ben Heineman fixed his attention on Toledo, Peoria & Western (TP&W), a 242-mile pike stretching from Effner, Indiana, on the Indiana–Illinois border through Peoria to Keokuk, Iowa, on the Mississippi River, with a spur to Lomax in western Illinois where TP&W connected with the main line of Atchison, Topeka & Santa Fe. TP&W was one of M&StL's favored partners through the Peoria Gateway, and acquisition of it would lengthen average hauls and extend M&StL's strategic options. But Heineman's methods were ham-fisted, and in the end TP&W passed to joint ownership by Pennsylvania Railroad and Santa Fe.

Success in expansion, denied in the TP&W case, came easily in 1956 when M&StL captured Minnesota Western, a 112-mile short line that stretched westward from Minneapolis to Gluek on a profile approximately thirty miles north of M&StL's route through Winthrop and Morton. M&StL operated Minnesota Western as a wholly owned subsidiary; its name was changed to Minneapolis Industrial on September 8, 1959.

Late in 1956 President Albert Schroeder convinced M&StL's board of directors to send the road's three-unit FT and F2 diesel locomotives (until recently numbered 445, 545, and 147) to Electro-Motive Division of General Motors for the purpose of rebuilding them into popular and versatile single-unit 1,500-horsepower GP9s that would have multiple-unit capacity and would be perfectly compatible with the company's F7s. The two FTs and one F2 moved to LaGrange, Illinois, in order of acquisition and emerged in 1956–57 as 600 through 608, painted in the new red and white livery. Later came fourteen additional GP9s, numbered 700 through 713, arriving in the fall of 1958. Alcos were sold as the used locomotive market permitted, but many were put through the Cedar Lake shop and upgraded for multiple operation.

New GP9s, often mixed with F7s, frequently found themselves assigned to flagship trains 19 and 20 on the Cedar Lake–Bartlett yard main, hustling time-sensitive lading over the Peoria Gateway. And shortly after the 700s arrived, M&StL added trains 1 and 2, paired opposite 19 and 20 by a half day and carded on fifteen-hour schedules. Operation began on January 28, 1959.

On October 18, 1959, a special train left Minneapolis carrying M&StL officials and directors to Aberdeen, South Dakota, for a directors' meeting to be held at the First National Bank. The event was in keeping with Schroeder's philosophy that such important gatherings should be held in various locations around the system. The mood was relaxed; the business transacted was routine. The next directors' meeting was on January 28, 1960. Again the agenda was routine, merely routine.

Matters were hardly routine on April 7, 1960, when department heads and other key personnel were told abruptly that M&StL would become a part of Chicago & North Western if the stockholders of the two companies and the Interstate Commerce Commission agreed—a very likely prospect. Indeed, it was pro forma. C&NW termed the transaction "self liquidating" with M&StL's contribution to C&NW's net equaling the purchase price in only five years. At 12:01 A.M. on Tuesday, November 1, 1960, the Minneapolis & St. Louis Railway Company ceased to exist.

Protocols varied over time, but typically train 57 from Fort Dodge tied up at Estherville, as did train 60 from Winthrop, so tonnage could be exchanged to the benefit of shippers. Train 56 trundled through Langdon on this cold January day in 1954.

M&StL's D-842 had the charm of requiring only an engineer (no fireman) but had the liability of being able to shoulder only light tonnage. During the summer of 1954 it was assigned to the Denhart branch, on Tuesdays, Thursdays, and Saturdays all the way from Hampton to Denhart, and on Mondays, Wednesdays, and Fridays making a Belmond turn. Train 390 leaving Belmond, August 15, 1954.

M&StL at one time was famous for special passenger trains, but by the 1950s they were scarce and the company had little of its own equipment for such use. On May 23, 1954, it dolled up Alco 546 and set aside two of the Budd cars plus some borrowed equipment for a trip to New Ulm from Minneapolis to the great satisfaction of area rail enthusiasts. A brief stop was authorized at Hopkins.

More than halfway along its trek from Minneapolis to Des Moines, train 2 has made its daily call at Humboldt on this warm summer day in 1954. Train and engine crews seem to sense the presence of a photographer; the RPO clerk appears otherwise distracted. PHOTOGRAPH BY BASIL W. KOOB.

Ben Heineman spent little time out on the line, leaving that chore to John Devins and others in senior management. Led by Alco 745 and trailing a heater car, *100*, and the *Twin Cities*, Passenger Extra 745 West slows through Dallas Center, Iowa, in September 1955. PHOTOGRAPHER UNKNOWN.

The New Ulm Switch Job was called six days per week at Winthrop for a New Ulm turn and also handled local work at Lafayette and Klossner. In this way tonnage moved overnight from Minneapolis to New Ulm and New Ulm to Minneapolis, with connection via Winthrop. A busy day's work already accomplished, Alco 751 hoists tonnage out of the Minnesota River valley through the village of Klossner in the summer of 1957. Eastbound billings, virtually all of this train's lading, will be added during the night to train 98 at Winthrop. The URTX refrigerator car, second behind the locomotive, is filled with Kraft cheese from the New Ulm plant.

GE-26 was among cars reconfigured to handle passengers as well as mail, baggage, and express. By 1957 trains 7 and 8 ran on a daily-except-Sunday basis, which explains why train 8 was seen in daylight at Albia on October 20, 1957. PHOTOGRAPH BY WILLIAM F. ARMSTRONG.

Train 7 typically arrived at Ackley ahead of time, which gave the agent, Dan Knight, an opportunity in November 1957 to snap pictures of (left) crewman Eddie Howell, in front of GE-26, and on another day, (above) Bob Mitchell (conductor) and Grover Bechtel (engineer). PHOTOGRAPHS BY DAN KNIGHT.

GE-31 quietly slips into Minneapolis with an abbreviated consist from Watertown. Train 14, May 25, 1958. PHOTOGRAPH BY WILLIAM D. MIDDLETON.

By the late 1950s passenger extras were rare but not unheard of. This one, on March 16, 1958, took rail enthusiasts from Minneapolis to Hutchinson on newly acquired Minnesota Western. PHOTOGRAPH BY WILLIAM D. MIDDLETON.

Albert W. Schroeder (lower left) put great stock in Budd's RDCs, and postal authorities, standing in the doorway of the RPO section, approved the new equipment. But the RDCs proved to be ill-starred. PHOTOGRAPHER UNKNOWN.

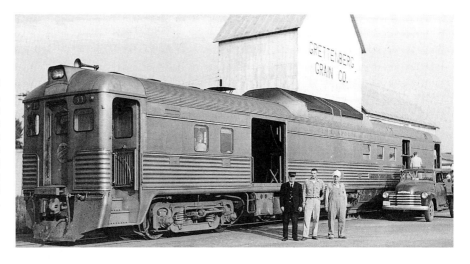

Self-contained RDC cars were designed to run by themselves without trailers, and that was the case for train 4 on June 15, 1958. By that time customers were scarce and the twenty-two seats in the passenger compartment usually more than met demand. RPO clerks continued to unload mail while the three-man train and engine crew posed beside RDC 33 at Perry, Iowa. PHOTOGRAPH BY BASIL W. KOOB.

M&StL's RDC4s were frequent visitors at the Cedar Lake shop, but on May 25, 1958, car 33 with trailer in tow performed flawlessly on the up trip from Des Moines on train 3, here shown coming into Minneapolis. PHOTOGRAPH BY WILLIAM D. MIDDLETON.

Train 4 was given a ten-hour schedule on the 310-mile overnight trip from Minneapolis to Des Moines, ample time for a short delay at St. Louis Park, Minnesota, for the photographer to make this memorable view on October 28, 1958. PHOTOGRAPH BY WILLIAM D. MIDDLETON.

The baggageman on trains 13/14 assigned to the Minneapolis–Watertown run had time to relax as the trains rolled along, but he was a busy fellow at thirty-six station stops where he was obliged to load and unload baggage, mail, and express. Train 13, early summer 1958. PHOTOGRAPH BY JOHN WINTER.

Not given the "passenger treatment" was GE-25, which, instead, was equipped for weed spray service—utilitarian and hardly glamorous. Deephaven, Minnesota, summer 1958. PHOTOGRAPH BY JOHN WINTER.

Early morning sun bathes train 14 at the Excelsior station on this day in June 1958. GE-27 was one of four cars equipped in 1957 by the Cedar Lake shop to handle passengers, who often commented unfavorably on the ride. PHOTOGRAPH BY JOHN WINTER.

Train 13 makes a flag stop at St. Louis Park on October 28, 1958. That community, located between Minneapolis and Hopkins, was named after M&StL, at the time usually referred to as "the St. Louis Road." PHOTOGRAPH BY WILLIAM D. MIDDLETON

Locomotives 608 and 600 get a roll on train 94 over M&StL's two-main-track line west of Cedar Lake Yard on May 4, 1958. With an early morning departure, 94's consist was made up of locally originated tonnage as well as cars from connections, especially Great Northern and Northern Pacific, that would be handed over to Illinois Central at Albert Lea and would roll eastward on an expedited basis as IC's AC-2. PHOTOGRAPH BY WILLIAM D. MIDDLETON.

M&StL steam lived on in 1958, not on M&StL but at the American Crystal Sugar plant at Chaska where Consolidation 452 was employed in October shunting carloads of beets that originated at outlying stations on M&StL and other roads. PHOTOGRAPH BY WILLIAM D. MIDDLETON.

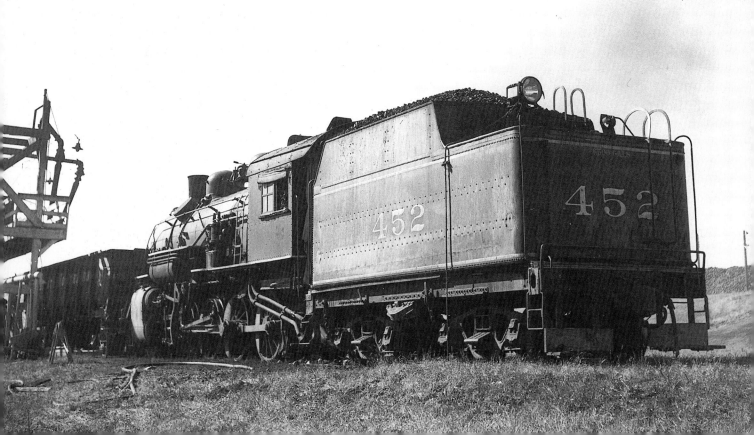

Cedar Lake shop was home to an accomplished band of M&StL employees who maintained the road's motive power fleet. October 20, 1958. PHOTOGRAPHS BY WILLIAM D. MIDDLETON.

Cedar Lake also served as M&StL's major classification yard in the Minneapolis area. At this location M&StL freight trains were made up or broken up; switch crews were on duty around the clock. Yard jobs often drew one of the road's many Alcos as motive power. October 13, 1958. PHOTOGRAPH BY WILLIAM D. MIDDLETON.

On October 27, 1958, train 95, headed by F3 403 and F7 406, broke the early morning silence as it approached Cedar Lake Yard with thirty-two cars gathered from the Wabash connection at Albia, from M&StL's own line to Fort Dodge and Des Moines, and from other main line stations. After setting out Cedar Lake tonnage, 95 will continue on through Lower Yard (west bank milling district) to St. Paul via Northern Pacific's "A" line. PHOTOGRAPH BY WILLIAM D. MIDDLETON.

Time freights 19 and 20 remained the company's pride and joy, expediting tonnage over the Peoria Gateway and giving M&StL a substantial division on overhead business. Train 20 is shown here at Cedar Lake Yard with Alcos in the background on October 29, 1958. PHOTOGRAPH BY WILLIAM D. MIDDLETON.

Train set, power on, and air tested, flagship train 20 is ready to depart Cedar Lake for its sprint to Peoria—ninety-nine loads, six empties, 5,380 tons led by four units of General Motors parentage (F3s, F7, GP-9)—on October 29, 1958. PHOTOGRAPH BY WILLIAM D. MIDDLETON.

Humble by comparison to M&StL's stable of time freights, the triweekly train on the Minnesota Western leaves Minneapolis over a stretch of Minneapolis, Northfield & Southern track at Glenwood Junction on October 13, 1958. On the point is nearly new 601 (ex-445B). **PHOTOGRAPH BY WILLIAM D. MIDDLETON.**

GE-29 during the late 1950s often found itself assigned to inspection trains such as this one with office car *Twin Cities* at Peoria in November 1958. PHOTOGRAPH BY PAUL H. STRINGHAM.

M&StL's locomotive roster included only two SD-7s, one of which usually found station at Peoria and the other roamed the system, often working the West End, but on October 27, 1958, was on duty at Cedar Lake. PHOTOGRAPH BY WILLIAM D. MIDDLETON.

New time freights 1 and 2 (Acey-Deucy) on the Cedar Lake–Peoria run opposite 19 and 20 were
the brainchildren of president Albert Schroeder. Train 2 made its initial departure from Cedar Lake
Yard on January 28, 1959. PHOTOGRAPH BY WILLIAM D. MIDDLETON.

The end of passenger service for M&StL between Minneapolis and Des Moines came on March 21, 1959, but at the request of the Post Office Department the company continued to run trains for mail service until April 19. On April 11, GE-31 rested at the Des Moines engine facility next to Alco 230 and GP-9 704.

In 1955 and later, Cedar Lake shopmen upgraded several of the Alcos for the purpose of operating them in multiple. This proved especially useful on the West End during the annual wheat rush and on the Fort Dodge–Spencer run where heavy tonnage in limestone and grain were frequent. On this warm early September Saturday in 1959, Alcos 225 and 207 lug a long train 56 through Gilmore City, Iowa.

Passenger Extra 405 West makes its exit from Great Northern's Minneapolis passenger station on Monday, October 27, 1958, with Northwest Bank's annual "Banco Special"—in this instance bound for Aberdeen, South Dakota—carrying bank managers and directors to visit satellite banks away from the Minneapolis headquarters. Consist: M&StL heater car, M&StL's 101, four Atchison, Topeka & Santa Fe sleepers, a Northern Pacific diner, and M&StL's *Twin Cities*. PHOTOGRAPHS BY WILLIAM D. MIDDLETON.

New GP-9s eventually bumped Alcos off their usual assignments such as trains 56 and 57 between Fort Dodge and Spencer. On this wintry day in January 1960, train 56 is led into Ayrshire, Iowa, by 606.

Snow was a perennial enemy to operations over much of M&StL's service territory. Long, shallow cuts on both sides of Raleigh in northwest Iowa presented predictable problems. Two Geeps were required to drive one of M&StL's Russell snow plows through drifts on an unusual horseshoe curve between Raleigh and Estherville after an ornery January storm in 1960. PHOTOGRAPHER UNKNOWN.

Train 50, the daily-except-Sunday freight from Albert Lea to Fort Dodge, is about to drop into M&StL's scenic path down Soldier Creek into Fort Dodge on this mild February Saturday in 1960. Note the two M&StL outside-frame 80,000-pound-capacity boxcars third and fourth behind the locomotive.

M&StL's earliest Iowa predecessor began life by linking Eldora and Steamboat Rock with Illinois Central at Ackley and hauling coal from beds along the Iowa River near this river crossing at Steamboat Rock. Train 20 ran in or near the valley of the Iowa River for over thirty miles. April 1960.

Train 13 had arrived in Watertown at 8:00 a.m. after its overnight trek from Minneapolis. The consist had been turned and would be allowed to doze before the handsome Watertown depot until departure as train 14 at 9:00 p.m. on April 21, 1960. PHOTOGRAPH BY WILLIAM F. ARMSTRONG.

M&StL had a very useful working relationship with Illinois Central on Minneapolis–Chicago freight traffic. Here is IC's AC-2 peeling off the joint track (M&StL, Rock Island, and IC) at Glenville, Minnesota (just south of Albert Lea), en route to Waterloo and then Chicago. The train had started at M&StL's Cedar Lake Yard at 9:30 a.m. and was handed to IC in Albert Lea at 12:30 p.m. Spring 1960. PHOTOGRAPHER UNKNOWN.

Train 14 paused at the Hopkins depot, 214 miles after leaving Watertown. The next stop is Great Northern's downtown Minneapolis station at 6:15 a.m. PHOTOGRA-PHER UNKNOWN.

In 1960 M&StL and IC divided power responsibly for their joint Minneapolis–Chicago operation, each company supplying one locomotive for each train operating between Waterloo and Cedar Lake. Here IC's AC-2 barrels over the Chicago Great Western crossing at Waverly, Iowa, in April 1960. Refrigerator cars just behind the locomotives carry Wilson & Company meat from Albert Lea.

Perhaps the final passenger special at M&StL was for rail enthusiasts to New Ulm and back to Minneapolis on April 24, 1960. M&StL supplied locomotive and heater car 501, but the rest of the equipment for the train had to be borrowed from other Twin Cities carriers. New Ulm. PHOTOGRAPHER UNKNOWN.

Marshalltown was the site for M&StL's impressive shop facility and yard. Flagship trains 19 and 20 often met there as was the case on this day (lower center right). PHOTOGRAPHER UNKNOWN.

This mellow late spring day at Chapin, Iowa, in 1960 was disturbed by the roar of M&StL's train 19
as it struggled upgrade from Hampton with a heavy haul bound for Cedar Lake Yard.

Alcos still ruled in South Dakota west of Watertown. On this warm summer day in 1960, train 116 wandered through the weeds near Florence.

Train 116 at Kampeska passes a fisherman, whose hat is visible at lower left. Behind the drawbar of Alco 210 are several carloads of wheat bound for the flour mills at Minneapolis in the summer of 1960.

A warm autumn sun shown brightly on train 56 as it rolled resolutely away from the tiny village of Langdon toward Spencer in October 1960.

The curtain fell for the last time on M&StL's regularly scheduled passenger service when trains 13 and 14 completed their respective runs on July 21, 1960. On the evening before, the crew out of Watertown posed for a newspaper photographer before a 9:00 p.m. departure. **PHOTOGRAPH BY** *WATERTOWN PUBLIC OPINION.*

M&StL sold Mogul 66 for scrap in 1942, but it ended up with an extended life on Missouri coal hauler Bevier & Southern. It rested between calls in this autumnal scene at Bevier, Missouri, on September 18, 1960.

By 1960, M&StL ran only twice weekly on the old Southwestern from Winthrop to Estherville (the New Ulm Switch Job worked six days per week on the Winthrop–New Ulm leg). On this dreary, gray day in October, train 60 lumbers by the depot at Dunnell, the last station in Minnesota before the line pressed into Iowa.

M&StL's massive neon sign and clock at the Minneapolis freight house belied reality. The sands of time for the "Tootin' Louie" would run out on November 1, 1960, when the property passed to Chicago & North Western.

What would happen to M&StL operations and what would happen to those who held jobs at Cedar Lake and the Railway Transfer in the west bank milling district of Minneapolis?

M&StL was justly proud of its Cedar Lake facilities and proud to promote expedited freight service through the Peoria Gateway. To that end a commercial photographer was hired to take this publicity view of new red-and-white diesel units with PBQ piggyback cars on the point. Shops and engine facility are at upper right with Kenwood's signature water tower in the background. PHOTOGRAPHER UNKNOWN.

Max A. Sedlmeier emigrated from Germany in 1914 and hired out as a brakeman for M&StL at Fort Dodge. He was promoted to conductor in 1919; as the curtain dropped on M&StL in 1960, he was the senior man at Fort Dodge. Sedlmeier signals "highball" for train 50 at Britt, Iowa.

End of the Line

The Minneapolis & St. Louis Disappears into the Chicago & North Western, 1960

MINNEAPOLIS & ST. LOUIS RAILWAY

"THEY RUN A RAILROAD a lot different than we [did]," exclaimed a bemused and irritated Clifford E. Ferguson, who in 1916 had hired on as a telegrapher at M&StL and by 1963 was Chicago & North Western's senior traffic representative at Peoria. Ferguson and a number of other former M&StL salesmen elsewhere had been retained by C&NW as were most train dispatchers and roadmasters, but survivors among operating managers and other senior officials were rare to nonexistent. Change in procedures and style were predictable, especially after a nasty strike against C&NW by the Order of Railroad Telegraphers in 1962. The Cedar Lake shop was closed, country depots by the dozens were shuttered, train service on branches was reduced, and line segments were abandoned. Time freights 19 and 20 surprisingly rolled on until April 11, 1968, but with their removal the former main line eastward from Oskaloosa, Iowa, stood in jeopardy (except in Illinois from Middle Grove to Peoria, because of active coal mines). It was abandoned in chunks from 1971 through 1976. It was much the same elsewhere. By the middle of the first decade in the twenty-first century, only bits and pieces of the old road remained in service—the most vibrant being the former main line from Albert Lea, Minnesota, to Manly and Marshalltown, to Eddyville in Iowa, as well as the former Central Division from Mallard to Grand Junction, Iowa. For that matter, Chicago & North Western had disappeared into the bowels of giant Union Pacific in 1995.

Sic transit gloria.

C&NW moved cautiously in the integration process, but a few changes occurred early. On the Southwestern, C&NW removed trains 60 and 61 on the Winthrop–Estherville run and used a Fort Dodge crew in twice-weekly operation from Fort Dodge to Hanska, Minnesota, 173 miles one way with twenty-four stations to be served. Crews hated the arrangement, dubbing it the "North to Alaska" job. An extra caboose was to lodge enginemen, but they took an exceedingly dim view of such accommodations. Extra 232 East rattled along near Terril, Iowa, in this scene from January 1961.

"North to Alaska" worked from Fort Dodge to Estherville on Mondays and Thursdays, a Hanska turn from Estherville on Tuesdays and Fridays, and Estherville to Fort Dodge on Wednesdays and Saturdays. January 17, 1961, was day 2. Crossing Chicago, Milwaukee, St. Paul & Pacific at Sherburn, Minnesota.

Southwestern tonnage to Minneapolis and east from Spencer to Hanska now was given to Chicago & North Western at St. James; billings from Lafayette, Klossner, and New Ulm were handed to C&NW at New Ulm. Former through service on M&StL via Winthrop was a thing of the past, and the line from New Ulm to Hanska was abandoned in place. But one last revenue trip was made on January 17, 1961, when "North to Alaska" brought a Milwaukee refrigerator car and an M&StL 80,000-pound-capacity boxcar to Hanska for the New Ulm Switch Job that handed the Fort Dodge crew eight empty grain boxcars to be distributed as it made its return run. This was the last time two trains met at Hanska; indeed, it was the last time a train moved over the line from New Ulm to Hanska. It presaged C&NW's intentions: remove one short segment to end through service and then abandon from each end. Soon the track from Klossner to New Ulm and from New Ulm to Hanska disappeared. It was like chopping off a dog's tail an inch at a time.

The New Ulm Switch Job enters Hanska for the final time on January 17, 1961.

Returned from Hanska, "North to Alaska" picked up a lengthy cut of boxcars from C&NW at St. James to be spotted at grain elevators at Echols, Ormsby, Monterey (Trimont), and Sherburn. Without a wye or turntable en route, the locomotive necessarily pointed short end forward. Approaching the Omaha (C&NW) crossing southwest of St. James on January 17, 1961.

Sixteen-hour days were routine for the "North to Alaska" run. It was time for a late dinner at Dunnell, Minnesota, on January 17, 1961. The crew was lucky to find an open beanery across the highway to the east.

C&NW quickly discontinued overnight freight trains 196 and 197 between Fort Dodge and Des Moines and instead instituted "as needed" service southward from Fort Dodge to Waukee. Brakeman Aldwin Erickson bounds out of the cab of locomotive 607 to wave a friendly greeting as the short train from Fort Dodge rolls by the depot at Waukee in March 1961.

Grain business from on-line stations south of Fort Dodge and connecting traffic from former M&StL lines at Fort Dodge usually resulted in heavy trains into Grand Junction where tonnage was handed over to C&NW. Here is Extra 608 East rolling down the hill from Dana into Grand Junction in the fall of 1961.

C&NW eventually terminated "North to Alaska" operation and took the Estherville–Terril line segment out of service–abandoning it in place, serving Langdon and Terril from the south and putting on a job from St. James that ran up to handle LaSalle and Hanska and south to Estherville. Business dwindled. Extra 231 West has only one car and a caboose as it makes the Dunnell station stop up from Estherville in August 1962. By now some former M&StL locomotives, like 231, have taken on the colors of Chicago & North Western, green and yellow.

C&NW did what it could to divert traffic from former M&StL lines to C&NW routings, but it also continued to operate trains 19 and 20 over the Peoria Gateway. On this day in the fall of 1962, units 709, 708, and 608—all in C&NW livery but with M&StL ancestry—roll 19's extra by the depot at Hopkins, only five miles short of its Cedar Lake destination.

Even before M&StL passed to C&NW, trains 1 and 2, "Acey-Ducey," were trimmed back from Minneapolis–Peoria operation, and C&NW continued to run them from Cedar Lake to Albia, usually handling heavy tonnage to and from C&NW at Marshalltown. Train 2's conductor picks up orders at Hopkins in October 1962.

Business in the Minneapolis west bank industrial zone remained good, especially to and from the flour milling facilities, with the result that former Railway Transfer (M&StL) crews still held several jobs at that location in October 1962.

A wonderful anachronism existed at Middle Grove, Illinois, where ex-M&StL 0-6-0s noisily toted coal to Midland Electric's tipple six days per week. Billings went eastward to Peoria over what had been M&StL's main line. March 1963.

Nemo, Illinois, had loomed large in M&StL's thinking. At that point, southeast of Monmouth, traffic to and from Atchison, Topeka & Santa Fe's main line was interchanged in great volume. By summer 1963 the volume was well off what it once had been, but trains 19 and 20 still made daily calls.

Peoria's Bartlett Yard was a mere shadow of its former self on June 16, 1963.

Business on the Albert Lea–Fort Dodge line remained strong during the mid-1960s, but track maintenance was not what it once had been. Train 50 is well off the advertised on this warm August day in 1966 when it drifted over the Winnebago River trestle into Forest City, Iowa. Conductor Raymond W. Dorn, on the walkway of locomotive 1765, soon will be directing switching at this important station stop. Note Alco 225 trailing.

C&NW honored the ancient traffic/operational agreement with Illinois Central Railroad for Minneapolis–Chicago traffic via Albert Lea, but C&NW did so without enthusiasm; after all, it had its own independent line between Minneapolis and Chicago. Here is a four-hour late 94 blasting through Hartland, Minnesota, in August 1966. Albert Lea and the Illinois Central connection is thirteen miles away.

Extra 1768 East with a mix of C&NW and former M&StL locomotives and with eight cars of feeder cattle and a long train of mixed freight (20's extra) roars by the joint C&NW and CRI&P depot at Northwood, Iowa, on an early September day in 1966. The relief agent gives the train a familiar highball signal.

Train 20 highballs out of Waterville, Minnesota, about equidistant between Minneapolis and Albert Lea, headed by three former M&StL units (607, 603, 608) and a C&NW Geep and trailed by a mile of cars in autumn 1967.

C&NW captured Chicago Great Western in 1968, and it was not long before CGW locomotives and other equipment appeared on former M&StL lines. Such was the case for this work extra in January 1969, a Russell plow headed by what had been M&StL's 705 and CGW 100C. Snow was not a problem at this location just south of Emmons, Iowa, on the Albert Lea–Fort Dodge line, but a little farther, around Lake Mills, cuts filled with drifted snow would present real challenges.

The M&StL sign over the diesel shop at Marshalltown long since had disappeared, but C&NW continued to use the facility for maintenance and repair in the summer of 1970. PHOTOGRAPH BY WILLIAM F. ARMSTRONG.

C&NW determined that most of the Denhart branch from Hampton through Belmond was redundant and abandoned it in place before actually seeking permission to tear out track. C&NW retained the 12.4-mile stub to Kanawha, using a former CGW crew from Belmond. Hampton, looking west over the CRI&P crossing, February 24, 1970. PHOTOGRAPHER UNKNOWN.

Foreign (not of M&StL origin) motive power increasingly appeared on former M&StL lines. F units such as this one teamed with an SD-9 seemed incongruous on the old Southwestern two miles north of Spencer during the summer of 1972.

M&StL's venerable fleet of RS1s gradually disappeared from road assignments. Such was the case on the St. James job where C&NW used one of its own Alcos for the up train from Estherville on August 10, 1976, just north of Dunnell, Minnesota.

As Chicago & North Western struggled during the 1960s and 1970s, one policy became clear: it would shed as many branch lines as possible. Did that policy include all former M&StL operations in the Fort Dodge area? That question remained unanswered during the summer of 1976 when this train trundled northward from Moorland, Iowa. The empty hoppers behind the drawbar of the second unit are bound for the limestone pits at Gilmore City.

Steam returned in dramatic form when Southern Pacific's elegant 4449 headed the 1976 *Freedom Train* through Hopkins. PHOTOGRAPH BY VERN WIGFIELD.

C&NW in 1976 abandoned and dismantled the line from Albert Lea to Lake Mills; the rest of the Albert Lea–Fort Dodge segment would perish in pieces between 1979 and 1985. But on this splendid summer afternoon in 1977, a Fort Dodge crew brought a few cars up to Forest City where bills were handed to the agent by the conductor.

Brakeman Don Messerly is about to alight from the locomotive of this southbound freight to pick up loads from the elevator at Curlew, Iowa, in the summer of 1977. The movement of grain in boxcars was nearing an end, and that reality would spell doom to many branches.

The Budweiser distributor at Spencer continued to ship by rail from St. Louis, and that helped sustain somewhat regular service from Fort Dodge to Spencer and up to Terril. When C&NW lost that business, a deep shadow rolled over much of that line. Southbound at Ayrshire in the summer of 1978.

The penultimate train makes its forlorn appearance at Terril, Iowa, to pick up a string of boxcars loaded with low-rated corncobs on July 19, 1981.

The last train on what had been M&StL's Southwestern Extension breaks the morning silence as it makes its way just north of Langdon en route from Terril to Spencer on August 11, 1981.

The final train from Spencer makes its way eastward over Milwaukee Road trackage, nearing Ruthven, from which point it will close out rail service to Ayrshire and Curlew. In this single abandonment, C&NW jettisoned 45.4 route miles and service to six communities. There was good news, however: the remaining route from Mallard through Tara to Grand Junction, 70 miles, would be rehabilitated to handle heavily ladened unit grain trains. August 11, 1981.

Sic transit gloria. North of Spencer, Iowa, in the fall of 1981.

Don L. Hofsommer is professor of history at St. Cloud State University in Minnesota. He is the author of many books on railroad history, including *The Tootin' Louie: A History of the Minneapolis & St. Louis Railway*, *The Great Northern Railway: A History*, *The Hook & Eye: A History of the Iowa Central Railway*, and *Minneapolis and the Age of Railways*, all published by the University of Minnesota Press.

Also Published by the University of Minnesota Press

The Boomer: A Story of the Rails by Harry Bedwell

Twin Cities by Trolley: The Streetcar Era in Minneapolis and St. Paul
    by John W. Diers and Aaron Isaacs

The Great Northern Railway: A History by Ralph W. Hidy, Muriel E. Hidy,
    Roy V. Scott, and Don L. Hofsommer

The Hook & Eye: A History of the Iowa Central Railway by Don L. Hofsommer

Minneapolis and the Age of Railways by Don L. Hofsommer

The Tootin' Louie: A History of the Minneapolis & St. Louis Railway
    by Don L. Hofsommer

Minnesota Logging Railroads by Frank A. King

The Missabe Road: The Duluth, Missabe and Iron Range Railway by Frank A. King

Union Pacific: Volume I, 1862–1893 by Maury Klein

Union Pacific: Volume II, 1894–1969 by Maury Klein

Dining Car to the Pacific: The "Famously Good" Food of the Northern Pacific Railway
    by William A. McKenzie

Rails to the North Star: A Minnesota Railroad Atlas by Richard S. Prosser

The 400 Story: Chicago & North Western's Premier Passenger Trains
    by Jim Scribbins

The Hiawatha Story by Jim Scribbins

Milwaukee Road Remembered by Jim Scribbins